The Use of Computers in Education Worldwide

Results from the IEA 'Computers in Education' Survey in 19 Educational Systems

INTERNATIONAL STUDIES IN EDUCATIONAL ACHIEVEMENT

Other titles in the series include

GORMAN, PURVES & DEGENHART

The IEA Study of Written Composition I: The International Writing Tasks and Scoring Scales

TRAVERS & WESTBURY

The IEA Study of Mathematics I: Analysis of Mathematics Curricula

ROBITAILLE & GARDEN

The IEA Study of Mathematics II: Contexts and Outcomes of School Mathematics

BURSTEIN

The IEA Study of Mathematics III: Student Growth and Classroom Processes

ANDERSON, RYAN & SHAPIRO

The IEA Classroom Environment Study

ROSIER & KEEVES

The IEA Study of Science I: Science Education and Curricula in Twenty-Three Countries

POSTLETHWAITE & WILEY

The IEA Study of Science II: Science Achievement in Twenty-Three Countries

KEEVES

The IEA Study of Science III: Changes in Science Education and Achievement: 1970 to 1984

The Use of Computers in Education Worldwide

Results from the IEA 'Computers in Education' Survey in 19 Educational Systems

WILLEM J PELGRUM
University of Twente, The Netherlands

TJEERD PLOMP
University of Twente, The Netherlands

Published for the International Association
for Educational Achievement by

PERGAMON PRESS

OXFORD · NEW YORK · SEOUL · TOKYO

U.K.	Pergamon Press plc, Headington Hill Hall, Oxford OX3 0BW, England
U.S.A.	Pergamon Press, Inc., 395 Saw Mill River Road, Elmsford, New York 10523, U.S.A.
KOREA	Pergamon Press Korea, KPO Box 315, Seoul 110-603, Korea
JAPAN	Pergamon Press, 8th Floor, Matsuoka Central Building, 1-7-1 Nishishinjuku, Shinjuku-ku, Tokyo 160, Japan

First edition 1991

Library of Congress Cataloging-in-Publication Data

Pelgrum, Willem J., 1950-
The use of computers in education worldwide : results from the IEA ''Computers in education'' survey in 19 educational systems / Willem J. Pelgrum, Tjeerd Plomp. -- 1st ed.
p. cm. -- (International studies in educational achievement)
Includes bibliographical references (p.).
1. Education--Data processing. 2. Educational surveys.
I. Plomp, Tj. II. Title. III. Series.
LB1028.43.P45 1991   370'.285--dc20   91-9968

British Library Cataloguing in Publication Data

Pelgrum, Willem J.
The use of computers in education worldwide : results from the IEA ''Computers in education'' survey in 19 educational systems. — (International studies in educational achievement).
1. Education. Use of computers
I. Title II. Series III. Plomp, Tjeerd IV. International Association for Educational Achievement
371.334

ISBN 0-08-041382-X

Printed in Great Britain by BPCC Wheatons Ltd., Exeter

Foreword

The International Association for the Evaluation of Educational Achievement (IEA) was founded in 1959 for the purpose of conducting international comparative studies of achievement of school students. IEA's aim is to study achievement against the wide background of school, classroom, home, student, and societal factors in order to enhance learning within and across systems of education. IEA has grown over the years to a cooperative of more than 40 research institutes, which studies have covered a wide range of subject matter areas.

IEA decided in 1985 to start the "Computers in Education" study. In stage 1 of this study, data were collected (in 1989) at national, school and teacher level. The first (descriptive) results of this stage are reported in this book. Other results of stage 1 will appear in national reports, in a research volume, and in articles in scholarly journals. The second stage of the study, with data collection in 1992, will be a follow-up of stage 1 and will also include measures of student outcomes in the domain of computer use in schools (functional computer knowledge and skills).

By publishing this book, IEA is further implementing its policy of reporting about the results of its studies soon after data collection. This study was planned with the expectation of publishing its first report one and a half year after data collection. Although IEA still can improve the logistics of its studies, it is satisfactory to observe that the international coordination of the study, under the leadership of dr. Willem J. Pelgrum, has been such that the original planning could be realized.

A study like this one is a costly enterprise. IEA is extremely grateful to the following organizations which contributed to the financing of the international overhead of the study: Ministry of Education and the Institute for Educational Research (SVO) of the Netherlands, Commission of the European Community (Brussels), National Institute for Educational Research (NIER) of Japan and the Japan Society for the Promotion of Science (JSPS), and the National Science Foundation of the USA. The Japanese contribution through NIER and JSPS has been received from Fujitsu Ltd., Hitachi Ltd., IBM Japan Ltd., Matsushita Electric Industrial Company Ltd., and Sony Corporation. Contributions were also received from Philips and IBM in the Netherlands.

IEA highly appreciates the great efforts of the staff of the International Coordinating Center of the study, located at the Department of Education, University of Twente, Enschede (the Netherlands) in preparing this book.

Tjeerd Plomp (Chairman IEA)

Preface

The IEA Computers in Education survey started in 1987 after preparatory work in the three preceding years. The main data collection took place in 1989 in 22 educational systems. This report contains a description of part of the data from 19 educational systems. The main Volume containing a description and analyses of stage 1 data will be published in 1992.

A project like this could not have been conducted without the help of many people from all over the world.

Our thanks go to the National Project Coordinators (whose names are listed in Appendix A), who altogether collected data from 60.000 respondents in their educational systems. We also greatly appreciate the efforts of all those colleagues who assisted in the preparatory work for this project, such as Dieter Kotte, Marlaine Lockheed, David Smith, Ron Ragsdale, as well as our assistants in the earlier days Cora Visser and Anke Steerneman.

The permanent members of the Steering Committee, Mr. Ryo Watanabe from the National Institute for Educational Research in Tokyo and Dr. Richard M. Wolf from Teachers College at Columbia University in New York contributed greatly to the study in all its stages.

Finally, in the preparation of this book many persons at the International Coordinating Center played an important role : Leendert van Staalduinen (data management); Ria Marinussen, Arjan Schipper and Wim Tielen (data processing); Ingeborg Janssen Reinen (co-author chapter IV and VI); Albert Tuijnman and Alfons ten Brummelhuis (Appendix E, LISREL analyses). Monique Kole did most of the layout work and the graphics, Maria Driessen designed the cover.

A special word of thanks we owe to Richard M. Wolf, who considerably improved the Dutch English of the main authors of this book.

Willem J. Pelgrum
Tjeerd Plomp

Contents

APPENDICES

Abbreviations

Throughout this book the following abbreviations for the participating educational systems are used:

BFL	Belgium-Flemish
BFR	Belgium-French
CBC	Canada British Columbia
CHI	China
FRA	France
FRG	Federal Republic of Germany
GRE	Greece
HUN	Hungary
IND	India
ISR	Israel
JPN	Japan
LUX	Luxembourg
NET	Netherlands
NWZ	New Zealand
POL	Poland
POR	Portugal
SLO	Slovenia
SWI	Switzerland
USA	United States of America

Readers should consult Appendix B for information about population definitions, representativeness of samples and sample sizes.

Chapter I
Theoretical framework, design and sampling

This chapter contains a short description of the background and theoretical framework of the study reported in the chapters that follow. The design and instrumentation is described as well as the sample sizes for each category of respondents in the educational systems that participated in the study. This chapter ends with an outline of the content of the book.

Aims and character of the study

Many countries throughout the world are facing issues about the role of computers in education: what is the place and role of computers in the schools? Is there a need for separate courses in computer literacy and computer science? How can the computer be used effectively in existing subjects? What will be the effect of computers on student learning, on teachers' behavior, on the school and classroom organization? These are important questions and, at present, we have little information to guide us in answering them. Moreover, the introduction of computers in education is probably the first major educational innovation which can be studied systematically almost from its earliest state of development.

These considerations led the International Association for the Evaluation of Educational Achievement (IEA) in 1985 decide to embark on an international comparative study of 'Computers in Education' (Comped) in which, at two points in time, data would be collected regarding the content and outcomes of this innovation in more than 20 educational systems. The Comped study is designed as a two stage study. Stage 1, with data collection in 1989, was aimed at collecting data at the national, school and teacher level. It was a survey, primarily descriptive in nature, focusing on how computers are currently being used, the extent and availability of computers in schools, the nature of instruction about computers, and estimates of the effects that computers are having on students, the curriculum and the school as an institution, as well as other factors influencing the use of computers in schools.

The second stage of the study, with data collection scheduled for 1992, will consist of two parts. The first part is a follow-up of stage 1, for studying changes over time. The second part of stage 2 will consist of assessing effects of school variables, teacher and teaching variables on student outcomes in the domain of computer usage in schools (functional computer knowledge and skills).

In principle, both stages are designed as studies, in which countries may decide per stage to participate.

More specifically, the aims of stage 1 of the Comped study were (Wolf, Plomp & Pelgrum, 1986):

1. to obtain information about the current status of the use of computers in education, more specifically within schools, which should serve as a valuable source of information for policy makers, teachers, administrators and other educational personnel engaged in planning, implementation and evaluation in the field of computers in education; and
2. to collect baseline information for studying in stage 2 directions of changes and developments in computer usage in education, as well as for analyzing relationships among various factors concerning the use and application of computers in education.

This preliminary report presents the first results of stage 1 of the Comped study. Other results will appear in a research volume to be published in 1992, in national reports of the participating countries, and in articles in scientific journals.

An important criterion for selecting the issues reported in this book is the potential relevance of data for policy makers at all levels in the educational systems of participating countries: national, state, regional, local and school level.

In the remainder of this chapter we will give a brief description of the context of the study by providing an overview of the type of arguments for introducing computers in education, and a summary of research findings, which illuminates the difficulties of integrating computers in the schools' curriculum. Next, the conceptual framework and the design of stage 1 of the study will be summarized, followed by an overview of the remainder of the book.

Why are new technologies important for schools?

Many reasons have been presented for introducing computers in education. Hawkridge (1990) summarizes these in four rationales.

Social rationale: children should be prepared to function adequately as citizens in a society permeated with new technologies.

Vocational rationale: children should be prepared to function adequately as professional workers in a technological society. Although the need for well prepared professionals is a societal need, this rationale is called vocational to clearly distinguish it from the preceding one.

Pedagogical rationale: computers may improve the instructional processes and learning outcomes.

Catalytic rationale: the use of computers may accelerate another educational innovation like more emphasis in the teaching and learning process on information handling and problem solving, and less on memorizing facts; this rationale refers to the possibility that schools can be changed for the better by the introduction of new technologies. Hawkridge (1990) and others refer to possible effects such as improved administrative and managerial efficiency; more emphasis on students learning by collaborating rather than by competing. In this approach computers are seen as catalysts, enabling desired change in education to occur (o.c., p.5).

Hawkridge (1990) points to two other rationales, which have at present little support in education. The *information technology rationale* supports the idea of stimulating national computer industry by placing at the government's expenses large numbers of nationally produced or assembled computers in the schools. Finally, the *cost-effectiveness rationale* argues that computers can reduce the cost of education drastically as they will allow for reducing the number of teachers. This rationale has indeed some validity in the domain of (corporate) training in business and industry, but is not really supported in formal education.

In addition to Hawkridge, one might distinguish especially in an early stage of computer introduction, an *opportunistic rationale* consisting of the expectation that the use of computers in schools may contribute to attract more students to the school.

Although Hawkridge presents these rationales as possible answers to the question why Third World countries may want to put computers in their schools, many educators and policy makers in other countries will recognize similar rationales when they recall the discussions on national, regional, local and/or school level about the introduction of new technologies, in the recent past predominantly computers, in education.

It is usually not one single rationale which guides policy makers. Often two or three of these rationales are simultaneously referred to as the starting points for policies at whatever level. On the other hand, the selection of one or more rationales as being the dominant ones, may determine to a large extent the implementation strategies as well as the budgets needed.

Why is it difficult to integrate computers in the school curriculum?

The introduction of computers in education is a large-scale complex innovation in which many obstacles need to be overcome before a successful implementation can take place. When designing the study during 1985-1987, it was known that in many countries the number of computers in schools had increased considerably over the years (Cerych, 1982). Yet, it was reported that little progress had been made in integrating computers in existing lesson practices: few teachers were actual users, software use was often restricted to drill and practice activities, the integration in the curriculum was poor (for example, Becker, 1986; Inspectorate, 1986).

Van den Akker, Keursten & Plomp (in press) reviewed the research (of both survey and case study type) and concluded that there was still a long way to go before computer use would be effectively integrated in most schools and classrooms. They concluded that there are four categories of important obstacles for a successful integration of computers in education: national context, school organization, external support, and innovation (product) characteristics.

National context: difficulties may arise if, apart from obvious tasks as investing in hardware, software development, research, teacher training and the like, there is a lack of proclamation of new aims for the educational system and encouragement "from above" for initiatives and activities in the field.

School organization: difficulties may arise if:
- there is a lack of encouragement and support from school administrators and principals, especially in the provision of facilities for training, acquisition of hardware and software, rearrangements of time tables, and other organizational measures;
- the school climate is negative and teachers are not mutually supportive by exchanging ideas and experiences and by providing feedback;
- there is no computer coordinator available;
- there is no long term security of supply and maintenance of hardware and software.

External support: many in-service training programs emphasized too much the technical aspects of computers while paying too little attention to the integration of computers into daily classroom practice and to skills in selecting and evaluating courseware. Teachers need strong support to overcome their (initial) problems of uncertainty and their concerns about changing teacher/student relationships and about accountability. There is a growing consensus about characteristics of in-service training that can increase its effectiveness: appropriate balance between theory and (guided) practice; detailed curriculum guides and plans for the course plus lesson-related materials and hand-outs; clear training objectives; in-service lessons linked to teachers' own instructional practice; peer interaction, including communication during hands-on activities; strategies for teaching heterogeneous groups; follow-up support and guidance.

Innovation characteristics: important concerns and questions related to characteristics of computers for the educational practice are:
- need and relevance: is there a need for using computers? How appropriate are computers for realizing certain goals? What is the priority of introducing computers in comparison with other concerns?
- clarity: how clear are the goals and the essential features of computer use for those who are supposed to work with computers? How clear are the practical implications for the users?
- complexity: how many components of instructional practice are affected, and how drastic are the deviations from existing practice and beliefs? How difficult is it to get familiar with the expected changes?
- quality and practicality: how well developed and tested are the software products? To what extent is the expected impact guaranteed? What is the trade-off between actual benefits and the personal and organizational costs?

These question are often asked by teachers (and other educational practitioners), who are ultimately the central actors in successfully implementing computers in educational practice. Weaknesses in one or more of the categories referred to above may cause major obstructions in the implementation of computers in educational practice.

Conceptual framework

In order to determine which information needed to be collected in this study, a framework was developed which identified the key factors at which the study was aimed. The framework consists of concepts derived from systems theory, curriculum theory and theories on educational change, as discussed in the previous section.

An educational system is a complex of subsystems at different levels: at the macro level the educational system of a country or state, at the meso level the school, and at the micro level the classroom and the student. On each level, educational decisions are influenced by different actors; for example, at the school level the school board, the principal, the subject matter department, and the teacher. External influences may be exerted by, for example, business and industry, or parents. The output of a subsystem at a certain level can be conceived as the input for the subsystem on the next level. For example, the output at the macro level may consist of policies, intentions and plans of governments, laid down in official documents, or existing as shared conceptions of what is expected from schools. Conceiving this as the input for schools, the output at this level consists of the activities and the practices in the classrooms, the time allocations and the instructional practices with computers of teachers. This is the input at the micro level, resulting in activities, cognitive skills and attitudes of students.

In curriculum theories, a distinction is made between the intended, implemented and attained curriculum. The intended curriculum refers to the curriculum plans (at the macro level), which may be laid down in official documents or which may exist as shared conceptions of what the important curriculum content is. The implemented curriculum (at the meso level) consists of the content, time allocations, instructional strategies, etc. which the teacher is actually realizing in his/her lessons. The attained curriculum (at the micro level) is defined as the cognitive skills and attitudes of students as a result of teaching and learning.

Taking these three curriculum levels as major input/output categories one may wonder how these levels influence each other and which factors may explain the occurrence of discrepancies. The literature on educational change may be used for tracing potential factors (e.g. Fullan, Miles, & Anderson, 1988). As already mentioned in the previous section, these factors include the quality, clarity and relevance of the objectives and the characteristics of the innovation (content, materials, instructional strategies); support and leadership; staff development; experiences with innovations; and the existence of evaluation and feedback.

This study incorporates the three different perspectives which are described above. The global conceptual framework for the study, in which the three perspectives are related to each other, is depicted in Figure 1.1.

The framework in Figure 1.1 identifies the actors who operate at different levels of decision-making in an educational system. The framework assumes that the decisions taken at different educational system levels influence each other via the curricular products which can be identified at each level. The curricular outputs at the macro and meso level can be conceived as mechanisms for directing the outcomes at student level. Different processes (indicated as influencing factors), derived from the literature on educational change, mediate and determine the characteristics of the curricular products at several levels. The picture illustrates that different sub-systems interact (sometimes mediated via other sub-systems) and that the "behavior" of a certain sub-system can only be understood if context information about "neighbor" sub-systems is available.

Certain factors in the model may be at the same time relevant as primary variables and as context variables. For example, the implemented curriculum may be important in itself when studied from an implementation perspective, but at the same time it may be conceived as context information when one is interested in studying student outcomes.

We have characterized the educational system in terms of levels of decision-making and the factors contributing to effect changes.

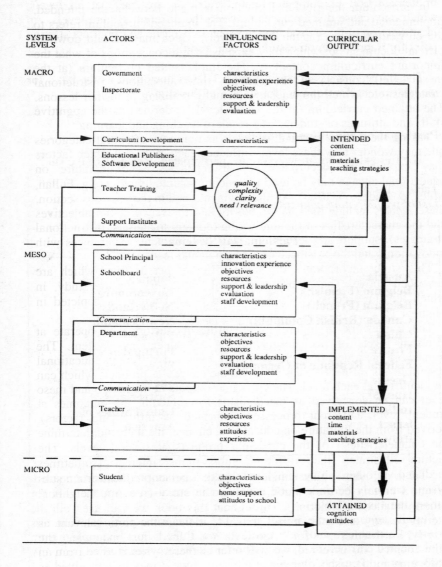

Figure 1.1. Global conceptual framework of the study.

The framework reflects the hierarchical structure of most educational systems, but acknowledges that decisions which promote or inhibit the implementation of computer-related curricula are made at all levels, which may cause discrepancies between the different system levels. An identification of these discrepancies may in itself be an important starting point for improvement measures in education.

The framework as shown in Figure 1.1 has been used as the basis for the instrument development for stage 1 of this study.

Participating educational systems

The following educational systems participated in stage 1 of the study:

Table 1.1
List of participating educational systems

Participating Systems	
Austria	Japan
Belgium (Flemish)	Luxembourg
Belgium (French)	Netherlands
Canada (British Columbia)	New Zealand
China	Poland
France	Portugal
Federal Republic of Germany	Slovenia
Greece	Spain
Hungary	Switzerland
India	United States of
Israel	America
Italy	

Table 1.1 shows that sometimes more than one educational system from a certain country participated in the study (see Appendix A for more detailed information). Throughout this book we will use both the terms *country* and *educational system* to indicate the participants in this study. Furthermore, as for Yugoslavia and Canada just one region from the country was involved, we will refer to these systems as respectively Slovenia and British Columbia.

The results presented in this book are based on data from the educational systems above except from Austria, Italy and Spain for which data were collected later than in most other countries. It is expected that the data from these countries will be included in future publications.

Design: populations, samples and instruments

This section contains a description of the populations, samples and instruments as defined for stage 1 of this study.

Populations of schools and teachers

The populations of interest are located in (1) elementary, (2) lower secondary and (3) upper secondary education. In stage 2 of the study also data on student level will be collected, for which the following (student) population definitions will be used:

Population 1:	students in the grade in which the modal age is 10 years (if more than one grade has a modal age of 10 years, the grade with the largest number of 10 year olds should be taken)
Population 2:	students in the grade in which the modal age is 13 years (if more than one grade has a modal age of 13 years, the grade with the largest number of 13 year olds should be taken)
Population 3:	students in the final year of secondary education

The datum date of age is the middle of the school year.

The data collection in stage 1 was restricted to school and teacher level. Given the global goals of stage 1, namely to provide a description of the status of computer use on school level, it was decided that the data collection in stage 1 should be aimed at grade ranges which contain the stage 2 populations plus and minus one year for elementary and lower secondary schools and minus 1 year for upper secondary schools. This was in particular the case for school level questionnaires and computer education teacher questionnaires.

The following definitions of the populations of schools and teachers to be used in stage 1 are derived from the student population definitions given above:

Population 1 (elementary schools)
- *non using schools*: all schools which do not use computers for teaching/learning purposes in grades in which the modal age of students is 9, 10 or 11 years.
- *using schools*: all schools in which computers are used for teaching/learning purposes in grades in which the modal age of students is 9, 10 or 11 years.
- *computer using teachers*: all teachers in computer using schools who use computers or teach about computers in grades in which the modal age of students is respectively 9, 10 and 11.
- *non computer using teachers*: all teachers in computer using schools who don't use computers and do not teach about computers, but are teachers of grades in which the modal age of students is respectively 9, 10 and 11.

Population 2 (lower secondary schools)
- *non using schools*: all schools which do not use computers for teaching/learning purposes in grades in which the modal age of students is 12, 13 or 14 years.
- *using schools*: all schools in which computers are used for teaching/learning purposes in grades in which the modal age of students is 12, 13 or 14 years.
- *computer using teachers existing subjects*: all mathematics, science and mother tongue teachers in computer using schools who provide lessons in these subjects in which computers are used to rades in which the modal age of students is 13 years.
- *non computer using teachers existing subjects*: all mathematics, science and mother tongue teachers in computer using schools who provide lessons in these subjects (without using computers) to grades in which the modal age of students is 13 years.
- *teachers computer education*: all teachers in computer using schools who teach about computers to grades in which the modal age of students is respectively 12, 13 and 14.

Population 3 (upper secondary schools)
- *non using schools*: all schools which do not use computers for teaching/learning purposes in the final and penultimate secondary grades.
- *using schools*: all schools in which computers are used for teaching/learning purposes in the final or penultimate upper secondary grades.
- *computer using teachers existing subjects*: all mathematics, science and mother tongue teachers in computer using schools who provide lessons in these subjects in which computers are used to students who are in their final year of secondary education.

- *non computer using teachers existing subjects*: all mathematics, science and mother tongue teachers in computer using schools who provide lessons in these subjects (without using computers) to students who are in their final year of secondary education.
- *teachers computer education*: all teachers in computer using schools who teach about computers to students who are in their final or penultimate year of secondary education.

In order to simplify the presentation throughout the rest of this report we will assume that the grade levels in which the modal ages of students are 10 and 13 are respectively grade 5 and 8 and that consequently the grade ranges which need to be considered for elementary and lower educational schools are 4-6 and 7-9.

Samples of schools and teachers

The sampling design for this study, as developed by the International Coordinating Center (ICC), can be summarized as follows:

> *The population of interest was stratified according to dimensions relevant for each participating educational system (and laid down in national sampling plans to be approved by the project's sampling referee). Minimum sample sizes for using and non using schools (if appropriate) were specified. Oversampling of certain categories of schools was allowed. Schools were selected with probabilities of selection proportional to the size of the school. The selected schools were asked to provide lists of names of the target groups of teachers as defined above. Next, National Centers selected teachers according to specifications provided in a sampling manual.*

For some countries it appeared to be necessary to deviate from this plan for technical and/or practical reasons. For instance, sometimes equal probabilities of selection were used, as it was not possible in some countries to sample schools with probabilities of selection proportional to the size of the school. Such deviations were negotiated with and approved by the International Coordinating Center (after consultation of the sampling referee) before they could be incorporated in a national sampling plan. Appendix B contains an overview of the samples per educational system reported. Table B.1 shows an overview of the realized samples per educational system. This table should also be consulted for inferring the number of cases on which the calculations for each of the tables in the following chapters are based. In order to compensate for different probabilities of selection of schools, weights were calculated and applied for all the school level results reported in this booklet, except for the Federal Republic of Germany and British Columbia for which information for weight calculations was not yet available at the time of preparing this report. This omission is assumed not to affect any of the conclusions reached in this booklet, as comparisons of weighted and unweighted statistics for the other countries did not change the major trends. All teacher results are unweighted.

Furthermore, the reader should note that due to the weights that are applied in this book, percentages should be read as reflecting the percentages of schools/teachers in the sample. Applying weights that reflect the student body represented may increase or decrease certain statistics depending on the correlation between school size and the variable of interest. For example, Table 2.1 (in Chapter II) contains the percentage of schools using computers for instructional purposes. We found that, if one would apply weights that reflect the student body represented by these schools, the percentage increases with up to roughly 10 % in lower secondary schools in Switzerland and Portugal.

Table B.1 shows that the sample sizes for computer using schools are in general quite acceptable, except for Greece because only about 5% of the schools in the country use computers. Although the number of schools in Luxembourg may look small, the sample constitutes the whole population.

The number of computer using teachers is rather small for many countries, especially when broken down by subject. This is due to the fact that in those countries only a small group of teachers (in mathematics, science or mother tongue) uses computers for their lessons.

For most countries, the samples of elementary and lower secondary schools are representative for the whole educational system, with the exception of Switzerland (where out of 26 cantons three were excluded for lower secondary schools and one for upper secondary schools) and the Federal Republic of Germany where not all the Bundesländer took part in this study. For upper secondary schools, the national representativeness of the samples is more often problematic. Some countries (like India and China) selected a few areas/cities, whereas other countries excluded certain school types. For instance, in the Netherlands in upper secondary schools, only teachers from general secondary eduation are presented and not from vocational or technical education. An overview of the excluded populations is given in Appendix B.

A further comment about the category "undetermined" in Table B.1 needs to be made.

The determination of users and non-users in this table was based on a definition containing a large number of items from each questionnaire. The category "undetermined" contains cases for which there is no evidence from the questionnaires whether computers are used or not.

Instruments

As indicated above, the instrumentation for this study was developed on basis of the framework in Figure 1.1 and finalized after pilot testing in 1988.

Table 1.2 contains an overview of the questionnaires for each population. The school and teacher questionnaires contained a part for computer users as well as non computer users. It should be noted that the teacher questionnaires for the three existing subjects have the same content except for the specification of the subject area and one question about the topics for which computers are used.

Table 1.2
Available instruments per population

Population	Instrument	Respondent
	National questionnaire	National Project Coordinator
1	School questionnaire	Principal
	Technical questionnaire	Technically informed person
	Teacher questionnaire	Teacher grade 4-6
2	School questionnaire	Principal
	Technical questionnaire	Technically informed person
	Teacher questionnaire subject[*]	Subject teacher grade 8
	Teacher questionnaire computer education	Teacher computer education grade 7-9
3	School questionnaire[**]	Principal
	Technical questionnaire[**]	Technically informed person
	Teacher questionnaire subject[*]	Subject teacher final grade
	Teacher questionnaire computer education	Teacher computer education final/penultimate grade

Notes. *: subjects are: mathematics, science and mother tongue, **: probably in most countries integrated with population 2 version.

The technically informed persons mentioned in Table 1.2 will be further referred to as computer coordinators.

Outline of this booklet

Chapter II contains a description of the availability of computer hardware and software in elementary, lower secondary and upper secondary schools. The results show that in most countries many secondary schools have access to computers, but that there are large differences between schools within countries as well as between countries in the number of available computers and the amount of available software. The lack of sufficient hard- and software is still seen as a major problem by a large group of educational practitioners.

Chapter III shows how the use of computers differs between countries. Moreover, the reasons of schools to start using computers and the purposes of current computer use will be identified. This description may give some indications about the directions of developments in countries that are still in an early stage of introducing computers in education and also indirectly indicates the needs of schools and teachers.

Chapter IV deals with staff development and shows what kind of staff development is available in the different educational systems and which topics are covered in the training teachers received. This chapter also contains the results of teachers' self-ratings of their knowledge and skills in handling computers.

Chapter V acknowledges that the introduction of computers in education is a major and complex innovation that can only succeed if - amongst others- the participants agree that it is worthwhile to be involved in this innovation. The data collected shed some light on the question how school principals and teachers think about the relevance of computers. The results show that in general principals and teachers have positive attitudes towards the educational impact of computers, but also that a great need for training exists.

Chapter VI deals with gender issues in relation to computers. Gender of principals, computer coordinators and teachers, being possible role models for students, is reviewed as well as special gender policies of schools, if they exist. The results show that computer use is mainly male dominated. Only in French-speaking countries many schools do have a special policy concerning gender issues.

Chapter VII contains a summary and discussion of the major findings reported in this booklet.

The content of most of this book is descriptive in nature. However, in order to offer the reader a perspective on the future work resulting from this project, we have included in Appendix E the results of explanatory analyses with LISREL for which the model specifications were derived from the theoretical framework presented in this chapter.

References

Akker, van den, J. J. H., Keursten, P. & Plomp, Tj. (in press). The integration of computer use in education. *International Journal of Educational Research.*

Becker, H.J. (1986). *Instructional uses of school computers: reports from the 1985 national survey: issue no 1, June 1986.* Baltimore: Center for Social Organization of Schools, The John Hopkins University.

Cerych, L. (1982). *Computeronderwijs in zes landen* [Computer Education in Six Countries]. Europees Instituut voor Onderwijs en Sociale Politiek van de Europese Culturele Stichting.

Fullan, M.G., Miles, M.B. & Anderson, S.E. (1988). *Strategies for implementing microcomputers in schools: the Ontario case.* Ontario: Ministry of Education, Queen's printer.

Hawkridge, D. (1990). Computers in third world schools: the example of China. *British Journal of Educational Technology,* 21 (*1*), 4-20

Inspectorate, (1986). *Een beschrijving van de stand van zaken in het schooljaar 1985/1986* [A description of the status in the school year 1985/1986]. Inspectierapport 7, deel 1 en 2. Ministerie van Onderwijs en Wetenschappen, Onderwijs en Informatietechnolgie.

Wolf, R., Plomp, Tj. & Pelgrum, W. J. (1986). *IEA Computers in education: design and planning.* Enschede (the Netherlands): University of Twente, Department of Education.

Chapter II
The availability of computer hardware and software

This chapter contains a description of the availability of computer hardware and software in elementary, lower secondary and upper secondary schools. The results show that in most countries many secondary schools have access to computers, but that there are large differences between countries as well as between schools within countries in the number of available computers and the amount of available software. The lack of sufficient hard- and software is still seen as a major problem by a large group of educational practitioners.

Do schools have access to and are they using computers?

During the 1980's in many educational systems throughout the world computers have been introduced in schools. However, national policies regarding the introduction of computers in education differed between countries: some countries do have clear policies of national governments, others are highly decentralized; some countries can be considered as forerunners (starting with the systematic large scale introduction of computers in education in the early 1980's), while other countries started in the late 1980's. Also the emphasis on certain educational levels differed between countries.

The differences in national policies are partly reflected in the number of schools in a country that had access to computers in 1989. Table 2.1 shows the percentage of schools having access to computers and their use for instructional or administrative-purposes-only. The classification of a school as user or non user was based on a decision scheme utilising information from questionnaires received from each school in the sample. For the interpretation of the figures in Table 2.1 it is important to note that respondents were asked to answer the questionnaires for certain grade ranges (for elementary schools: grade 4-6; lower secondary schools: grade 7-9; upper secondary schools: the final and penultimate year of secondary education).

In **elementary education** the access to computers is low in Japan and Portugal (respectively 25% and 29%), moderate in Belgium-French (54%), Israel (62%), the Netherlands (53%), while a high degree of access at school level can be observed in British Columbia (99%), France (92%), New Zealand (78%) and the USA (100%).

In **lower secondary education** in Belgium-Flemish, Belgium-French, British Columbia, Federal Republic of Germany, France, Luxembourg, the Netherlands, New Zealand, Switzerland and the USA three quarters or more of the schools have access to and use computers for instructional purposes; Greece, Japan and Portugal show low or moderate access rates of respectively 5%, 36% and 53%.

Most **upper secondary schools** in the educational systems that participated in this study have computers, while access to computers is still low or moderate in Greece (4%), the sampled provinces/cities in China (61%) and India (7%).

If computers are available in schools, they are used for instructional purposes by most schools.

Table 2.1
Percentage of schools using computers per educational system

Country / Educational System

Use of Computers	BFL	BFR	CBC	CHI	FRA	FRG	GRE	HUN	IND	ISR	JPN	LUX	NET	NWZ	POL	POR	SLO	SWI	USA
Elementary schools																			
No use	-	40	0	-	8	-	-	-	-	38	68	-	46	21	-	69	-	-	0
Instructional	-	54	99	-	92	-	-	-	-	62	25	-	53	78	-	29	-	-	100
Only administrative	-	6	1	-	0	-	-	-	-	0	7	-	0	1	-	1	-	-	0
#respondents	0	243	154	0	367	0	0	0	0	260	329	0	217	470	0	243	0	0	425
Lower secondary schools																			
No use	7	1	0	-	1	5	95	-	-	-	56	0	13	0	-	45	-	22	0
Instructional	78	93	100	-	99	94	5	-	-	-	36	100	87	99	-	53	-	74	100
Only administrative	15	6	0	-	0	1	0	-	-	-	7	0	0	1	-	3	-	4	0
#respondents	280	187	138	0	416	409	385	0	0	0	318	27	259	123	0	256	0	938	415
Upper secondary schools																			
No use	0	2	0	39	0	0	96	0	93	18	1	-	31	0	28	27	4	2	0
Instructional	98	93	100	61	99	100	4	100	7	82	94	-	69	100	72	72	94	98	100
Only administrative	1	5	0	0	1	0	0	0	0	0	4	-	1	0	1	1	2	0	0
#respondents	264	191	138	376	380	197	456	311	872	184	563	0	214	134	566	214	78	322	425

Note. - = data not collected.

Table 2.1 also shows that the group of schools that use computers only for administrative purposes is small in most countries. Exceptions are Belgium-Flemish, Belgium-French and Japan where, respectively, 15%,

6% and 7%, of the lower secondary schools belong to this category.

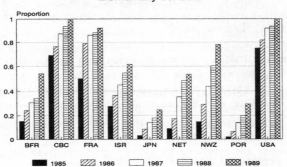

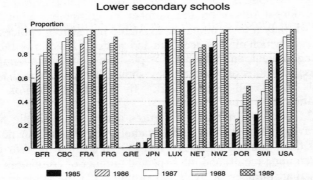

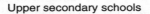

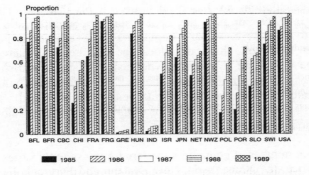

Figure 2.1. Proportion of schools having computers over the years.

Figure 2.1 shows for each level, the percentage of the schools having computers in the years 1985-1989. From these figures it seems reasonable to expect that the number of schools having access to computers will increase rapidly for those countries where the access rate in 1989 was far below the 100%.

As the results that are presented below are mainly focused on the computer-using schools, Table 2.1 also furnishes an impression of the percentage of schools in an educational system to which the generalizations, that will be made in most of the following sections, apply.

How many computers do schools possess?

The way computers can be used in the teaching/learning process depends amongst others on the number of computers available in a school. With only a few computers available in a school choices need to be made as to which classes, teachers and students are allowed to use the available equipment, and whether it is possible to integrate computers in whole class activities or whether they should be applied on the basis of individual or small-group work by students and/or teacher demonstrations in front of the class.

Table 2.2 shows a number of figures about the available hardware schools having computers in 1989, namely (1) the median number of computers those schools possessed in 1989, in each of the four previous years (based upon recall) and the expected number of computers in 1990, (2) the median number of available printers, (3) the student:computer ratio, (4) the median year schools started with introducing computers for instructional purposes and (5) the median number of computers not in use. The calculations are based on those schools that had at least one computer in 1989. For 1989 the median student:computer ratio has been included to indicate how many computers are available for how many students in a school. This index does not indicate how many students actually have to share a computer when using it (such a statistic will be presented in Chapter III) and, hence, this statistic could be an overestimate. Also the median of the year schools started with using computers is included as an indicator of the history of this innovation in an educational system.

The median number of computers in **elementary schools** varies between 2-4 in France, the Netherlands, New Zealand and Portugal, 10 in Japan and respectively, 17, 18 and 16 in British Columbia, Israel and the USA.

Table 2.2
Medians of number of computers over years, year of first use, number of computers not used in 1989 and number of printers (according to computer coordinators)

Country / Educational System

Use of Computers	BFL	BFR	CBC	CHI	FRA	FRG	GRE	HUN	IND	ISR	JPN	LUX	NET	NWZ	POL	POR	SLO	SWI	USA
Elementary schools																			
First year	-	86	83	-	85	-	-	-	-	86	87	-	87	87	-	86	-	-	83
1985	-	0	2	-	1	-	-	-	-	0	0	-	0	0	-	0	-	-	4
1986	-	2	4	-	1	-	-	-	-	8	0	-	0	0	-	0	-	-	7
1987	-	3	7	-	1	-	-	-	-	12	2	-	1	1	-	1	-	-	9
1988	-	5	12	-	1	-	-	-	-	16	7	-	2	1	-	2	-	-	12
1989	-	5	17	-	2	-	-	-	-	18	10	-	2	2	-	3	-	-	16
1990	-	7	19	-	2	-	-	-	-	21	12	-	2	3	-	4	-	-	17
Student:computer ratio 1989	-	28	21	-	23	-	-	-	-	17	14	-	64	62	-	301	-	-	23
# computers not used	-	0	0	-	1	-	-	-	-	0	0	-	0	1	-	0	-	-	0
# printers	-	1	4	-	1	-	-	-	-	1	3	-	1	1	-	1	-	-	4
Lower secondary schools																			
First year	84	84	82	-	85	85	88	-	-	-	87	83	84	83	-	87	-	87	83
1985	-	3	8	-	6	7	0	-	-	-	0	10	6	6	-	0	-	0	7
1986	-	5	14	-	8	8	0	-	-	-	0	14	8	10	-	0	-	2	10
1987	-	7	21	-	10	9	0	-	-	-	1	15	10	11	-	2	-	6	12
1988	-	10	33	-	12	10	0	-	-	-	3	16	13	13	-	4	-	7	15
1989	12	12	43	-	15	11	8	-	-	-	7	16	18	17	-	5	-	9	18
1990	13	15	56	-	17	13	8	-	-	-	9	31	19	20	-	6	-	11	21
Student:computer ratio 1989	27	34	12	-	31	46	52	-	-	-	143	48	26	34	-	287	-	21	17
# computers not used	0	0	0	-	3	2	0	-	-	-	0	0	0	1	-	0	-	0	0
# printers	2	3	9	-	2	3	1	-	-	-	2	3	2	3	-	2	-	3	4
Upper secondary schools																			
First year	83	82	82	86	83	80	86	83	86	84	85	-	83	82	87	86	85	83	82
1985	5	5	8	0	4	6	0	3	0	8	2	-	8	8	0	0	1	7	12
1986	7	6	14	11	8	8	4	6	2	10	8	-	11	11	0	0	3	10	15
1987	9	7	21	13	12	10	8	11	2	12	14	-	15	13	4	2	7	13	20
1988	10	10	33	20	18	12	8	14	2	16	21	-	21	14	6	4	8	15	21
1989	12	11	43	23	24	14	17	17	2	20	25	-	25	18	10	5	11	19	27
1990	14	14	56	30	30	16	17	18	2	24	27	-	26	20	11	7	16	25	33
Student:computer ratio 1989	32	38	12	43	26	48	44	28	572	26	32	-	34	37	53	289	58	20	14
# computers not used	0	0	0	0	3	2	0	1	0	0	0	-	0	1	0	0	1	0	0
# printers	3	3	9	2	7	4	3	2	1	2	13	-	5	4	2	2	2	7	10

Notes. - = data not collected, 1985-1988: recall; 1989: actual; 1990: expected.

British Columbia and the USA show a steady increase over years, whereas in Japan there is a sudden increase in 1988. In other countries, the number of computers in elementary schools is more or less stable over years. Sudden increases may reflect the effect of governmental programs for equipping schools with computers. In most countries elementary schools started quite recently with the introduction of computers (typically more than 50% of the schools started in or after 1986) with the exception of the USA where the median starting year was 1983. The student:computer ratio varies substantially between about 15-25 in British Columbia, Israel, Japan, France and the USA and almost three to four times as many in countries like the Netherlands and New Zealand. Exceptional is Portugal with a student:computer ratio of 301, which is caused by the fact that Portuguese elementary schools are quite large. It is interesting to note that the student:computer ratio in France suggests a more favorable picture for elementary schools than the absolute number of available computers. This can be explained by the relatively small school size of elementary schools in France (with a median of 71 students compared to, for instance, 233 in Belgium-French and 830 in Portugal).

The median number of computers in **lower and upper secondary schools** is in general higher than in elementary schools. Comparing the first year of educational computer use across populations, one finds a stable trend of upper secondary schools starting first, followed by lower secondary schools and the last the elementary schools. However, the differences between countries are quite large, showing for instance that many educational systems were, in 1989, at the level of the USA and British Columbia in 1985 or 1986 with respect to the median number of computers in schools. Although one may observe from Table 2.2 that in most educational systems secondary schools acquired more computers over years, the increases are quite different, showing for instance that upper secondary schools in British Columbia and the USA not only have the highest number of computers available, but also that these numbers are still increasing which leads to the expectation that these education systems will stay in this position in the forthcoming years, if the policies of other countries remain unchanged.

On the whole, the student:computer ratio tends to be more favorable in secondary schools than in elementary schools. There are however, again, large differences between countries, showing that in the USA the conditions for integrating computers in the school curriculum are most favorable, while in other countries the ratio's are almost two to three times as high. It is also interesting to note that, although Switzerland has a relatively low number of computers per school, the student:computer ratio is quite favorable (and almost at the level of the USA) due to the fact that Swiss schools on the average are relatively small.

One of the questions arising from the results presented in this section is whether schools have enough computers. This question is difficult to answer from a theoretical perspective because so many factors are involved, such as the goals of computer use, availability of adequate software, training of teachers, etc. However, we may get a tentative answer to this question by looking at the problems educational practitioners perceive as serious in using computers.

One of the questions presented to all respondents (principals, computer coordinators and teachers) contained a list of about 30 problems (related to hardware, software, teacher training and skills, and organization) which could be experienced as serious in using computers for educational purposes in the school. Respondents were asked to check each problem that they considered as serious in using computers in the school, but also to select from the list the five most serious problems. Table 2.3 contains the percentages of school principals and computer coordinators that indicated a particular hardware problem in their top five selection from the total list of problems.

From Table 2.3 (and also from the full problem lists in Appendix D) we may infer that the lack of a sufficient number of computers and peripherals (although less frequently mentioned) is perceived as a serious problem by a large group of respondents in many countries. Overall, across countries, the patterns of percentages from principals and computer coordinators are quite similar, although there are also some exceptionally high discrepancies such as, for instance, in Luxembourg in lower secondary schools.

Some further inspection of the data revealed that there is no linear relation between the frequency of identifying a lack of hardware as problematic and the student:computer ratio. A first tentative explanation for this might be that a number of other factors probably affect the perception of respondents as to what are the major problems in using computers. It may be, for instance, that even with a low number of available computers in combination with a low number of teachers who are knowledgeable enough in using the available hardware, principals or computer coordinators may perceive a lack of hardware as less problematic than the lack of sufficient opportunities for training teachers. On the other hand, a relatively large number of computers may be perceived as insufficient in schools where many teachers are interested in using computers in their lessons.

In some countries (for instance, in lower secondary schools in Belgium-Flemish, France, Germany, Luxembourg, Portugal and Switzerland) relatively large groups of respondents complain about the limitations of computers (like being out of date). This may be related to the type of computers available in the schools (see next section).

Table 2.3
Percentage of school principals (P) and computer coordinators (C) including a particular hardware problem in their top-five selection of serious problems in using computers in school

Country / Educational System

Hardware Problem		BFL	BFR	CBC	CHI	FRA	FRG	GRE	HUN	IND	ISR	JPN	LUX	NET	NWZ	POL	POR	SLO	SWI	USA
Elementary schools																				
Insufficient computers	P	-	52	64	-	54	-	-	-	-	36	46	-	73	69	-	63	-	-	58
	C	-	58	61	-	46	-	-	-	-	34	29	-	70	65	-	67	-	-	54
Insufficient peripherals	P	-	10	26	-	8	-	-	-	-	13	18	-	16	24	-	17	-	-	37
	C	-	13	22	-	8	-	-	-	-	21	15	-	24	29	-	21	-	-	32
Difficulty maintenance	P	-	8	16	-	30	-	-	-	-	14	0	-	0	13	-	3	-	-	6
	C	-	6	15	-	26	-	-	-	-	14	4	-	1	11	-	2	-	-	10
Limitations of computers	P	-	4	10	-	25	-	-	-	-	18	12	-	21	5	-	8	-	-	12
	C	-	12	16	-	23	-	-	-	-	29	18	-	15	5	-	20	-	-	11
Lower secondary schools																				
Insufficient computers	P	43	50	53	-	37	18	32	-	-	-	50	17	37	62	-	70	-	40	63
	C	33	34	32	-	36	22	14	-	-	-	61	26	33	38	-	68	-	31	52
Insufficient peripherals	P	21	14	27	-	7	5	13	-	-	-	15	13	14	24	-	27	-	14	37
	C	20	16	8	-	4	16	13	-	-	-	11	11	11	18	-	28	-	7	24
Difficulty maintenance	P	2	5	10	-	18	3	16	-	-	-	4	13	7	14	-	3	-	4	8
	C	4	7	4	-	22	8	23	-	-	-	5	48	9	20	-	5	-	9	11
Limitations of computers	P	13	5	7	-	18	12	8	-	-	-	9	26	2	8	-	11	-	14	15
	C	16	9	10	-	18	24	8	-	-	-	9	30	10	13	-	21	-	22	16
Upper secondary schools																				
Insufficient computers	P	44	51	53	54	49	19	-	36	59	44	47	-	44	53	31	72	54	28	65
	C	41	39	33	42	38	14	-	24	59	41	46	-	28	43	21	69	m	26	50
Insufficient peripherals	P	32	16	27	35	18	8	-	31	16	17	18	-	16	22	23	26	7	11	33
	C	27	17	8	33	16	12	-	32	16	19	16	-	9	18	21	31	m	6	19
Difficulty maintenance	P	4	4	10	29	16	3	-	16	23	16	9	-	11	12	35	4	11	12	8
	C	5	8	4	35	14	7	-	13	22	18	6	-	9	18	35	5	m	12	9
Limitations of computers	P	20	4	7	25	12	14	-	23	6	24	19	-	8	17	15	10	16	22	14
	C	19	10	11	38	11	24	-	29	10	28	17	-	13	14	14	17	m	31	18

Notes. - = data not collected, m = insufficient number of cases (n<50 or missing cases >20%).

Which types of computers do schools possess?

Beside the number of computers in a school, the type of available hardware is another important factor which may be of potential influence in determining how computers are used in schools. For instance, most of the current integrated software packages using windows and mouse techniques, can only be run efficiently on powerful computers equipped with at least 80286 or 68000 processors.

A first rough indication of the available types of hardware can be obtained by looking at the processor types of the machines that are available in the schools. Each participating school was asked to list the type/brand of each available computer and the number of computers of that type in the school. The type/brand was coded according to the following scheme: 1: IBM   8086, etc.; 2: Z-80, etc.; 3: other 8-bit processor; 4: IBM 80286, etc.; 5: Motorola 68000 ; 6: IBM 80386, etc.; 7: Motorola 68000+, etc; 8: other process. types. Categories 1-3 concern 8-bit machines, while categories 4-7 can be characterized as the more up-to-date machines. The categories were combined as follows:
8086, etc: category 1; 80286, etc: categories 4 and 6; Other 8-bit: categories 2 and 3; 68000, etc.: categories 5 and 7.

Figure 2.2 shows for each educational system and educational level the relative proportion of computers for each of these combined categories.

Figure 2.2 shows that in many countries in elementary schools the category "Other 8-bit"-processors predominate, while in secondary schools in most countries there are more machines equipped with processor types that are mainly used for IBM-compatible systems. Machines equipped with the more advanced processor types (such as the 80286 and 80386) are still rather scarce, although Japan is a clear exception.

Machines equipped with processor types that are typically used for Atari and MacIntosh machines only are available in relatively large numbers in lower secondary schools in Switzerland and in upper secondary schools in Greece, Hungary, Poland and Switzerland. The figures clearly illustrate the lack of standardization of hardware in many countries. One may hypothesize that in most countries this situation was caused by a lack of explicit national policies on introducing of computers in education, resulting in grass-root developments whereby each school determined its own policy for acquiring hardware. However, on the other hand, one may expect that (given the policies towards standardization of hardware that were adopted in recent years in many countries) standardization will increase in the near future.

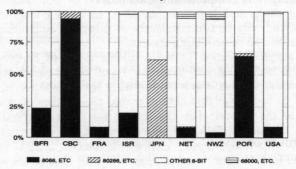

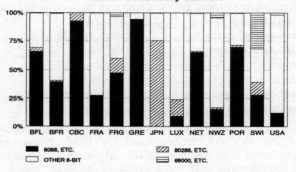

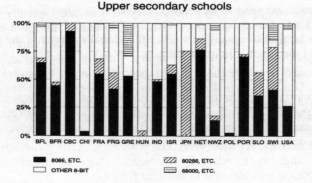

Figure 2.2. Distribution of processor types.

Which software is available in the schools?

The availability of instructional software is another necessary condition for using computers in schools. Therefore this survey contained a number of questions about the availability of software in the schools. The computer coordinators were asked to check which of the following types of programs were available in the school:

drill and practice	database
tutorial programs	lab interfaces: automatic
word processing	data acquisition
painting or drawing	programs to control devices
music composition	programs to control interactive video
simulation	CAD/CAM
recreational games	CAI authoring language
educational games	item banks
programming languages	record/score tests
spreadsheet	grade book
mathematics graphing	computer communication
statistics	tools/utilities

This is a total of 23 different types of software. As a first rough indicator of the variety of software available in schools we calculated for each school the percent of items checked in this list and next took the mean of these percentages per educational system. Figure 2.3 shows that there are large differences between educational systems in the variety of software types available in the schools.

An important distinction with respect to types of software is between general purpose software (like word processors, spreadsheets and data base programs) that can be used in different contexts and special purpose software developed for specific applications.

Elementary schools

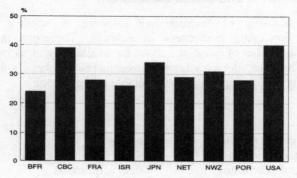

Lower secondary schools

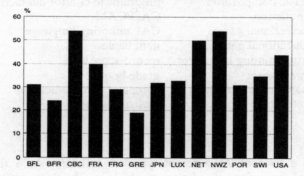

Upper secondary schools

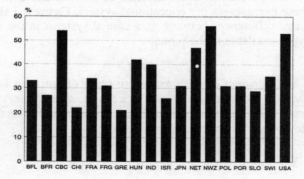

Figure 2.3. Average percentage of software types (see text).

Table 2.4 gives a more detailed overview of the types of software **elementary** schools possess.

Table 2.4
Percentage of computer using elementary schools having particular types of software (according to computer coordinators)

Country / Educational System

Type of software	BFR	CBC	FRA	ISR	JPN	NET	NWZ	POR	USA
Drill practice	85	92	89	98	94	82	83	38	98
Tutorial programs	41	79	27	49	62	43	60	20	84
Word processing	74	98	66	62	77	86	97	81	81
Painting drawing	34	65	75	53	77	54	47	71	39
Music composition	15	27	54	14	32	18	14	15	19
Simulation	20	51	19	23	38	20	47	7	48
Recreational games	40	38	70	41	48	76	72	61	60
Educational games	62	82	87	84	40	94	88	76	89
Programming language	71	68	85	69	54	25	18	60	34
Spreadsheet	22	61	30	15	40	31	28	64	44
Mathematical graphing	17	33	16	11	21	23	19	47	36
Statistics	4	16	6	3	23	8	8	20	13
Database	28	62	11	39	21	45	41	63	50
Lab interfaces	3	4	1	1	1	2	1	0	2
Control devices	6	2	3	1	2	0	15	2	11
Control interactive video	3	1	0	0	5	0	2	1	3
CAD/CAM	12	1	1	1	5	0	2	1	3
CAI authoring language	2	4	4	10	57	1	2	0	6
Item banks	4	13	1	32	6	12	3	2	19
Record/score tests	8	24	1	9	16	22	13	2	29
Gradebook	5	43	3	6	47	10	9	3	53
Computer communication	3	29	3	1	11	6	4	7	7
Tools/utilities	18	43	16	10	29	30	52	34	40

Table 2.4 shows that, except for Portugal, in most participating countries more than 80% of the computer using elementary schools possess drill and practice software. For tutorial programs there are large differences between countries: in the USA it is quite common for schools to possess these programs, whereas, for instance, in France only 27% of the schools have programs of this type. Word processing software and educational computer games are also available in many schools, although

the percentages for word processing found in France and Israel (respectively 66% and 62%) are relatively low. Databases and spreadsheets are less widespread. Furthermore, it is interesting to note that the availability of programming languages in elementary schools varies considerably between as well as within countries: about 70% or more of the schools in Belgium-French, British Columbia, France and Israel have programming languages available. This points to the potential use of LOGO (see Chapter III). On the other hand, Table 2.4 shows that in some countries (New Zealand, the Netherlands and the USA) only a small group of elementary schools (17-35%) possesses programming languages.

Table 2.5
Percentage of computer using lower secondary schools having particular types of software(according to computer coordinators)

Country / Educational System

Type of software	BFL	BFR	CBC	FRA	FRG	GRE	JPN	LUX	NET	NWZ	POR	SWI	USA
Drill practice	52	64	84	96	67	6	60	71	72	87	44	53	93
Tutorial programs	47	31	80	47	26	14	33	0	80	81	41	46	78
Word processing	88	77	99	91	88	84	66	92	98	99	88	97	91
Painting drawing	25	29	84	70	36	9	70	33	62	61	64	79	45
Music composition	4	6	45	37	4	5	9	4	7	37	6	30	24
Simulation	23	16	47	32	33	2	35	33	58	74	23	21	52
Recreational games	22	31	43	59	30	23	25	41	60	77	55	62	67
Educational games	27	37	78	78	21	9	22	30	70	92	45	38	93
Programming language	78	67	76	77	99	86	61	92	67	80	71	80	42
Spreadsheet	75	51	94	72	66	66	63	96	92	84	73	87	55
Mathematical graphing	41	39	48	52	50	8	25	63	74	76	45	33	36
Statistics	18	17	23	24	15	6	38	26	48	58	28	17	15
Database	74	46	91	55	64	77	55	92	92	84	74	81	56
Lab interfaces	8	5	11	5	18	2	3	11	16	8	4	1	7
Control devices	37	5	9	27	24	2	1	33	22	15	2	9	10
Control interactive video	0	0	8	1	0	2	3	0	0	1	1	1	4
CAD/CAM	23	14	44	5	4	2	5	0	16	26	4	10	11
CAI authoring language	9	2	10	28	6	2	56	0	81	13	4	6	10
Item banks	3	2	42	6	1	3	7	0	31	5	3	4	22
Record/score tests	6	3	45	7	1	13	14	0	26	45	5	9	33
Gradebook	23	4	89	28	1	2	79	0	42	75	1	19	62
Computer communication	12	9	62	8	8	3	11	19	24	27	10	11	12
Tools/utilities	37	19	69	46	29	28	32	37	57	83	45	36	42

In **lower secondary schools** the picture is somewhat different (Table 2.5). Software for word processing, spreadsheets and databases is widely available in most countries. The availability of database programs is relatively low in Belgium-French, France, Germany, Japan and the USA. Programming languages are also widely available in lower secondary schools, although the percentages of schools possessing programming languages are relatively low in Belgium-French, Japan, the Netherlands and the USA (respectively 67%, 61%, 67% and 42%). Drill and practice and/or tutorial programs are available in many lower secondary schools in some systems (British Columbia, New Zealand and the USA), but in a relatively small number of schools in other countries (for example, Belgium-Flemish, Greece, Portugal and Switzerland).

Table 2.6

Percentage of computer using upper secondary schools having particular types of software(according to computer coordinators)

Country / Educational System

Type of software	BFL	BFR	CBC	CHI	FRA	FRG	GRE	HUN	IND	ISR	JPN	NET	NWZ	POL	POR	SLO	SWI	USA
Drill practice	60	53	85	36	63	67	6	71	71	61	40	65	71	57	49	52	35	86
Tutorial programs	43	22	81	26	29	24	18	61	56	47	23	71	74	69	41	28	55	86
Word processing	98	88	99	27	94	85	67	81	90	72	69	99	100	61	87	88	91	99
Painting drawing	22	30	84	35	36	35	17	65	55	24	49	60	75	62	64	72	56	51
Music composition	3	5	45	25	8	3	0	45	51	8	6	3	31	35	8	5	12	27
Simulation	27	28	47	13	30	49	13	66	63	37	28	58	78	31	23	17	32	56
Recreational games	20	30	43	53	23	26	39	91	73	35	24	34	70	79	55	71	31	61
Educational games	15	26	78	27	31	17	7	66	66	48	16	38	74	64	44	30	20	84
Programming language	87	73	76	43	75	99	97	76	77	88	75	84	89	77	68	85	94	73
Spreadsheet	89	64	94	33	88	72	62	54	66	46	71	98	100	20	71	49	90	90
Mathematical graphing	55	40	48	15	56	64	17	59	71	21	22	56	82	56	45	33	40	52
Statistics	23	30	23	34	31	25	11	55	44	8	32	36	76	8	28	21	28	27
Database	86	63	91	29	78	57	57	63	73	35	58	97	96	41	77	67	83	83
Lab interfaces	6	6	11	2	14	26	0	11	8	6	3	19	14	6	4	10	7	18
Control devices	27	8	8	2	18	24	10	11	8	13	7	23	12	1	1	5	16	16
Control interactive video	1	1	8	2	4	1	0	6	3	1	2	0	3	0	1	0	1	11
CAD/CAM	24	13	45	7	27	3	6	12	11	10	15	27	27	1	5	10	26	28
CAI authoring language	15	7	10	7	17	9	0	1	6	11	36	56	9	12	4	5	6	21
Item banks	8	3	42	12	1	3	0	5	19	11	3	18	5	4	3	11	5	38
Record/score tests	7	2	45	19	4	2	27	16	16	4	24	16	45	6	5	13	8	38
Gradebook	33	10	90	57	15	1	3	29	4	16	83	51	89	9	0	7	16	70
Computer communication	11	8	62	2	9	13	4	13	4	4	17	32	32	8	8	0	26	23
Tools/utilities	35	28	70	29	46	31	31	38	21	17	34	69	92	33	45	18	50	54

Table 2.6 shows that many **upper secondary schools** (more than 70%) possess programming languages (China only 43%) and word processing programs (in China only 27%). A general trend is that in comparison with lower secondary schools the availability of drill and practice and tutorial programs is somewhat lower in upper secondary schools, but spreadsheets, databases and more specialized programs (like programs for controlling devices or CAD/CAM programs) are available in more schools.

The computer coordinators were also asked to indicate for which subjects software was available in the schools. Table 2.7 contains the percentage of coordinators indicating that software was available for a particular subject. The USA is not included in this table as the questionnaire item addressing this issue was not included as it was assumed that software for all subjects is easily available nationally.

Table 2.7 shows that a majority of **elementary schools** possess software for mathematics and mother tongue. However, software for informatics (that is, learning about computers) is not as widespread. In lower and upper secondary education many schools in the participating educational systems possess some software for courses to learn about computers (informatics) and for mathematics. There are, however, remarkable differences. For instance, the percentage of schools having software for mathematics in lower secondary education ranges from 10 % in Greece to 95 % in New Zealand and France. Similar differences are found for software that can be used in other courses, such as science and mother tongue.

An important question to address at this point is to what extent the availability of particular software might be an indicator of the way computers are used in a school. More specifically, one may wonder whether the availability of drill/practice and tutorial programs (which are usually subject-bound) is related to the integration of computers in existing subjects. Factor analyses show that a distinction can be made between general purpose software and more subject specific software. Moreover the correlation of factor scores with the number of subjects in a school in which computers are used showed that the availability of more subject specific software is associated with a broader use of computers in terms of the number of subjects for which computers are used. Thus, it seems that the availability of software is related to the type of use of computers in a school. The nature of this relation needs to be further investigated, as plausible arguments may be brought forward for claiming that causality operates in both directions.

Table 2.7
Percentage of schools having software for particular subjects (according to computer coordinators)

Country / Educational System

Subjects	BFL	BFR	CBC	CHI	FRA	FRG	GRE	HUN	IND	ISR	JPN	LUX	NET	NWZ	POL	POR	SLO	SWI
Elementary schools																		
Informatics	-	47	58	-	66	-	-	-	-	62	27	-	46	54	-	34	-	-
Mathematics	-	88	87	-	87	-	-	-	-	88	94	-	96	84	-	77	-	-
Science	-	27	59	-	39	-	-	-	-	17	62	-	12	25	-	27	-	-
Mother tongue	-	82	78	-	88	-	-	-	-	80	61	-	96	66	-	33	-	-
Foreign language	-	6	6	-	4	-	-	-	-	72	0	-	19	3	-	36	-	-
Creative arts	-	10	36	-	52	-	-	-	-	11	25	-	42	22	-	33	-	-
Social studies	-	39	67	-	47	-	-	-	-	21	51	-	89	44	-	33	-	-
Commercial studies	-	*	0	-	0	-	-	-	-	0	0	-	0	18	-	4	-	-
Technology general	-	2	17	-	13	-	-	-	-	0	0	-	0	1	-	2	-	-
Lower secondary schools																		
Informatics	92	69	76	-	71	72	66	-	-	-	27	78	91	87	-	54	-	72
Mathematics	52	54	67	-	93	82	10	-	-	-	66	63	89	95	-	57	-	51
Science	28	24	60	-	81	4	2	-	-	-	60	37	80	60	-	38	-	29
Mother tongue	24	37	64	-	91	32	2	-	-	-	27	4	85	80	-	15	-	23
Foreign language	43	20	13	-	81	23	2	-	-	-	39	4	75	30	-	23	-	24
Creative arts	2	4	47	-	57	6	2	-	-	-	12	0	38	27	-	18	-	13
Social studies	8	14	58	-	67	28	0	-	-	-	30	7	79	63	-	26	-	15
Commercial studies	35	29	67	-	31	26	2	-	-	-	0	37	59	79	-	42	-	30
Technology general	14	5	28	-	62	7	0	-	-	-	32	0	10	*	-	2	-	-
Technology specific	20	15	24	-	32	2	0	-	-	-	0	7	20	31	-	20	-	3
Home economics	4	0	21	-	14	0	0	-	-	-	14	0	3	15	-	1	-	1
Upper secondary schools																		
Informatics	93	65	75	52	67	73	56	81	85	72	51	-	84	91	82	54	83	68
Mathematics	58	54	67	43	63	89	13	83	74	53	38	-	58	92	75	53	41	35
Science	33	31	59	50	50	9	0	67	70	46	42	-	56	76	67	36	40	25
Mother tongue	14	23	64	5	50	32	0	22	15	32	10	-	52	68	18	13	12	9
Foreign language	45	19	13	29	45	23	0	60	11	39	17	-	53	24	49	19	13	10
Creative arts	7	5	47	9	15	7	0	17	20	7	5	-	19	29	22	17	0	6
Social studies	6	17	58	8	28	32	3	18	26	9	9	-	53	63	6	25	10	9
Commercial studies	51	34	68	12	61	20	10	14	24	46	29	-	45	86	3	41	22	42
Technology general	9	4	27	1	24	2	0	30	11	3	14	-	1	*	1	2	15	6
Technology specific	22	15	23	3	42	5	3	35	-	26	0	-	55	31	3	20	15	14
Home economics	7	0	21	1	7	1	0	2	2	1	16	-	0	6	14	1	0	2

Notes. - = data not collected, *: subject does not exist.

Is there enough software available?

This study did not record which programs are available in the schools, and whether there is any shortage of particular software, or what the quality of the available programs is. However, there are a few indicators that can throw some light on these questions. These indicators consist of the inventory of **problems** that were presented to the respondents with the request to indicate which problems with respect to software were experienced as serious in using computers.

Table 2.8

Percentage of principals (P) and computer coordinators (C) including a particular software problem in their top five selection of serious problems in using computers in the school

Country / Educational System

Software Problem	P/C	BFL	BFR	CBC	CHI	FRA	FRG	GRE	HUN	IND	ISR	JPN	LUX	NET	NWZ	POL	POR	SLO	SWI	USA
Elementary schools																				
Insuff. software	P	-	32	35	-	19	-	-	-	-	34	62	-	46	34	-	38	-	-	25
	C	-	54	32	-	21	-	-	-	-	47	75	-	57	45	-	48	-	-	32
Softw. difficult	P	-	2	1	-	5	-	-	-	-	1	3	-	3	4	-	1	-	-	5
	C	-	4	3	-	5	-	-	-	-	4	3	-	7	3	-	0	-	-	0
Softw.not adaptable	P	-	13	3	-	11	-	-	-	-	3	29	-	26	5	-	4	-	-	5
	C	-	13	3	-	11	-	-	-	-	5	23	-	19	4	-	7	-	-	4
Poor manuals	P	-	3	1	-	6	-	-	-	-	4	4	-	4	13	-	1	-	-	1
	C	-	4	2	-	6	-	-	-	-	2	8	-	6	8	-	3	-	-	2
Lack info softw.	P	-	5	7	-	13	-	-	-	-	9	14	-	6	15	-	3	-	-	9
	C	-	13	7	-	11	-	-	-	-	7	13	-	7	18	-	8	-	-	5
Softw.other lang.	P	-	2	8	-	1	-	-	-	-	3	0	-	3	3	-	6	-	-	0
	C	-	3	2	-	0	-	-	-	-	3	1	-	0	2	-	10	-	-	0
Lower secondary schools																				
Insuff. software	P	32	34	39	-	13	21	37	-	-	-	36	9	53	20	-	41	-	33	25
	C	50	38	27	-	18	30	55	-	-	-	65	59	53	34	-	55	-	37	36
Softw. difficult	P	3	1	0	-	4	5	6	-	-	-	7	0	10	1	-	2	-	5	1
	C	0	2	1	-	5	5	3	-	-	-	4	0	17	4	-	4	-	9	1
Softw.not adaptable	P	15	6	11	-	17	3	12	-	-	-	12	4	34	2	-	4	-	11	8
	C	25	10	3	-	13	4	10	-	-	-	14	4	20	5	-	8	-	12	9
Poor manuals	P	2	3	8	-	3	5	23	-	-	-	4	0	4	2	-	2	-	7	2
	C	8	11	7	-	4	9	41	-	-	-	7	0	6	5	-	8	-	13	5
Lack info softw.	P	6	12	11	-	14	5	17	-	-	-	10	18	6	7	-	7	-	8	4
	C	9	15	7	-	13	14	18	-	-	-	20	4	8	17	-	12	-	8	6
Softw.other lang.	P	8	4	2	-	0	0	27	-	-	-	0	26	2	1	-	3	-	4	0
	C	9	2	0	-	1	1	29	-	-	-	0	22	3	1	-	10	-	6	0
Upper secondary schools																				
Insuff. software	P	30	31	39	57	22	-	25	48	32	38	47	-	39	32	55	35	41	19	18
	C	36	35	26	58	23	-	26	47	34	40	44	-	44	25	56	55	m	28	30
Softw. difficult	P	2	1	0	0	1	-	4	4	3	0	7	-	4	0	1	1	6	8	0
	C	1	2	1	1	3	-	4	3	5	2	4	-	3	0	1	2	m	9	1
Softw.not adaptable	P	13	9	11	4	9	-	3	6	11	10	19	-	21	13	10	5	10	8	14
	C	15	5	4	4	7	-	3	6	11	8	17	-	17	9	6	7	m	4	8
Poor manuals	P	7	5	8	8	4	-	11	13	5	2	5	-	6	1	23	1	4	13	3
	C	13	6	7	6	6	-	8	19	7	9	6	-	6	5	30	7	m	14	5
Lack info softw.	P	8	16	11	8	10	-	8	8	10	13	11	-	6	10	11	8	6	8	12
	C	4	12	7	8	9	-	18	15	10	9	12	-	15	14	14	11	m	8	6
Softw.other lang.	P	4	0	2	10	1	-	0	6	13	5	3	-	2	0	5	3	2	3	0
	C	7	6	0	14	0	-	1	5	10	7	1	-	3	0	3	8	m	4	0

Notes. - = data not collected, m = insufficient number of cases (n<50 or missing cases >20%).

The data show (see Table 2.8 and Appendix D) that a shortage of software is experienced as a serious problem, while the lack of information about software or the adaptability of software is frequently mentioned as the second problem.

Table 2.9
Percentage of computer coordinators checking expenditures as important or very important

Country / Educational System

Expenditure	BFL	BFR	CBC	CHI	FRA	FRG	GRE	HUN	IND	ISR	JPN	LUX	NET	NWZ	POL	POR	SLO	SWI	USA
Elementary schools																			
More comp. in labs	-	42	78	-	20	-	-	-	-	62	29	-	20	2	-	64	-	-	44
More comp. in class	-	38	40	-	35	-	-	-	-	55	37	-	61	52	-	47	-	-	47
More powerful computers	-	22	33	-	20	-	-	-	-	65	35	-	35	13	-	49	-	-	19
Netwrk shared disk access	-	17	43	-	22	-	-	-	-	38	29	-	16	7	-	33	-	-	20
Netwrk instruct.softw.	-	14	39	-	12	-	-	-	-	55	38	-	12	7	-	32	-	-	25
More printers/other periph.	-	38	61	-	22	-	-	-	-	58	48	-	33	31	-	63	-	-	46
Greater variety software	-	67	67	-	52	-	-	-	-	90	90	-	86	71	-	76	-	-	73
More tool software	-	52	57	-	44	-	-	-	-	66	65	-	48	58	-	63	-	-	42
Lower secondary schools																			
More comp. in labs	47	66	81	-	34	27	56	-	-	-	49	75	41	51	-	60	-	40	51
More comp. in class	37	23	41	-	28	17	23	-	-	-	23	37	31	38	-	57	-	32	44
More powerful computers	33	33	36	-	38	50	26	-	-	-	36	71	16	35	-	56	-	41	23
Netwrk shared disk access	14	15	70	-	37	28	16	-	-	-	32	13	30	26	-	42	-	24	22
Netwrk instruct.software	15	10	52	-	24	24	28	-	-	-	40	13	18	14	-	46	-	14	25
More printers/other periph.	47	44	52	-	28	55	46	-	-	-	45	42	44	36	-	68	-	42	40
Greater variety software	80	64	64	-	64	74	63	-	-	-	75	63	92	66	-	77	-	69	64
More tool software	62	54	56	-	52	69	65	-	-	-	70	50	59	62	-	65	-	56	47
Upper secondary schools																			
More comp. in labs	44	68	82	64	42	32	38	51	65	76	44	-	44	52	45	59	45	49	51
More comp. in class	38	21	42	7	54	11	20	32	25	25	21	-	31	36	25	53	44	29	44
More powerful computers	41	41	36	38	41	57	53	66	48	71	46	-	33	37	50	50	77	54	26
Netwrk shared disk access	22	15	70	22	18	29	49	55	28	45	34	-	30	28	27	40	36	33	27
Netwrk instruct.software	16	15	52	27	17	22	34	42	29	51	34	-	14	17	1	44	35	26	21
More printers/other periph.	39	52	52	38	53	53	41	61	58	64	60	-	37	42	58	69	60	41	39
Greater variety software	72	61	64	52	53	73	45	83	68	89	74	-	81	60	85	75	44	66	58
More tool software	51	59	57	47	70	70	42	65	73	72	65	-	50	48	69	64	77	66	49

Note. - = data not collected.

The observation from Table 2.8 is consistent with the priorities for computer-related expenditures mentioned by computer coordinators (see Table 2.9), showing that in most countries and across populations the most frequently mentioned priority is a greater variety of instructional software.

Why are schools not using computers?

The question addressed in this section may, at first sight, look trivial for countries where the possibilities for schools to acquire computers are rather limited (due to for instance a lack of local or central governmental financial resources). This may be true for developing countries, but in most developed countries this argument is hard to maintain given the low prices of computers (relative to the budgets of schools). In situations were school budgets are under pressure, schools may set other priorities for their expenditures than the acquisition of computers. On the other hand, from the perspective of equal opportunities for students to get acquainted with new technologies, the question may be raised as to why, in certain schools, computers are still not being used. A partial answer to this question comes from Tables D.12 - D.14 (Appendix D). These tables contain, for those countries with access rates considerably below 100%, the percent of principals including a particular reason in their top five selection of reasons for not using computers in the school. The results in Tables D.12.- D.14 show that the lack of knowledge of teachers and organizational/financial constraints are mentioned by large groups of respondents in many countries.

What do the results show?

The results described so far show that once computers are available in schools they are used for instructional purposes. The results constitute a snapshot of the situation that existed in 1989. Some tables showed that rapid changes occurred between 1985 and 1989 in the percentage of schools that had access to computers. The average number of computers in schools changed more gradually although in some countries sudden jumps can be observed as a result of (governmental) stimulation programs. Many educational practitioners still see a lack of software and hardware as the most important problems encountered in using computers. The LISREL analyses reported in Appendix E show that this perceived shortage is related to the degree of integration of computers in existing lesson practices. Moreover, there are clear indications from the reasons for not using computers that a lack of knowledge on the part of teachers is seen as an important problematic issue (see also Chapter IV and Appendix D).

Chapter III
Why and for which purposes are schools using computers?

Given the limited number of available computers in schools in many countries, as reported in the previous chapter, one may not expect that the use of computers in schools around the world is already widespread among many subjects and teachers. However, some countries are much further ahead of other countries and, therefore, a description is given as to how the use of computers differs between countries. This chapter will also describe why schools started using computers and for what purposes the equipment is currently used. Moreover, the changes teachers perceive as a result of using computers and the problems they experience will be addressed.

Why are schools using computers?

From the first days of the introduction of computers in schools, many claims have been put forward about the possible advantages and disadvantages of using computers. These claims ranged from statements about the beneficial effects of learning LOGO or other programming languages on logical thinking or problem solving skills to claims about the expected increase of educational efficiency and productivity. Educational practitioners are exposed to these claims (for which the empirical evidence is not spectacular) and may have adopted some of them as reasons for introducing computers in the school.

The school principals participating in this study were asked to rate the importance of each statement in a list of ten containing potential reasons for introducing computers in the school (the answer categories were: not important, slightly important, important and very important). The list consisted of the following statements: (1) students need experience with computers for their future; (2) computers make school more interesting; (3) computers attract more student to the school, (4) computers improve student achievement; (5) computers keep the curriculum up to date; (6) computers promote individualized learning; (7) computers promote cooperative learning; (8) the school had an opportunity to acquire computers; (9) the teachers were interested in and (10) a category "other reasons". A first inspection of the data showed that, with the exception of reason (2), a majority of respondents attached some importance to all of these reasons. However, in elementary schools in Belgium-French, Israel, Japan and Portugal about three quarter of the principals attached some importance to reason (2). In order to visualize the major trends with respect to the reasons for introducing computers more clearly, we collapsed the answer categories"important" and very "important" and calculated the percentage of respondents checking one of these answers. The results of this operation are presented in Table 3.1. In order to interpret these figures it is particularly revealing to compare the results between the different levels within school systems.

Table 3.1 shows that at all levels the expected improvement of student achievement is mentioned by a large majority of respondents. In elementary schools the promotion of individualized learning stands out as a reason to which a relatively high degree of importance is attached. Also revealing are the high percentages on reason (7), namely the interest of teachers, which illustrates that this innovation is also strongly "bottom up" and clearly anchored in the teaching force.

For which purposes are computers used?

Computers may be used for a wide variety of purposes in a school. In the past some different typologies have been presented to characterize the major distinctions in the type of use of computers, such as tutor-tool-tutee or learning with, learning about, and learning through computers. Schools, however are constrained in their use of computers due to a number of different factors, such as the shortage of hard- and software (see previous chapter), and the limited availability of teacher time (see also Appendix D). Also the capacity of computers may influence the type of use. The use of the earliest micro computers presupposed quite a lot of programming skills, while the newest versions hardly require more understanding than the conception of a computer as a black box.

In order to describe how computers are currently being used in schools, we first will make a rough distinction between learning about computers and the use of computers as teaching and/or learning aid.

Learning about computers is organized in schools in different ways. Table 3.2 shows that, in most countries, students in secondary schools acquire their operational skills in handling computers (like starting up, saving and loading of files, etc.) for a major part in separate courses that are part of the official school curriculum. However, in France only a minority of secondary schools have separate courses, but instead, most schools integrated the learning about computers into existing subjects. In case that there are no separate courses on computers in education, mathematics and vocational type of courses (commercial studies and specific technology) are usually the most frequently mentioned contexts in which learning about computers takes place.

Table 3.1
Reasons for introducing computers in schools (according to principals)

Country / Educational System

Reasons Introduction	BFL	BFR	CBC	CHI	FRA	FRG	GRE	HUN	IND	ISR	JPN	LUX	NET	NWZ	POL	POR	SLO	SWI	USA
Elementary schools																			
Experience for future	-	92	99	-	87	-	-	-	-	85	91	-	97	94	-	98	-	-	92
Make school interesting	-	86	71	-	68	-	-	-	-	84	82	-	41	76	-	95	-	-	65
Attract students	-	42	5	-	6	-	-	-	-	48	38	-	3	8	-	45	-	-	12
Improve achievement	-	86	71	-	54	-	-	-	-	86	73	-	75	79	-	88	-	-	80
Curric/method up-to-date	-	65	82	-	49	-	-	-	-	77	80	-	59	69	-	73	-	-	90
Individualized learning	-	89	78	-	66	-	-	-	-	91	95	-	78	82	-	74	-	-	73
Cooperative learning	-	81	43	-	63	-	-	-	-	57	55	-	47	81	-	73	-	-	46
Opportunity to acquire	-	70	56	-	40	-	-	-	-	45	81	-	56	40	-	70	-	-	52
Teachers were interested	-	82	84	-	50	-	-	-	-	73	68	-	89	78	-	87	-	-	63
Lower secondary schools																			
Experience for future	98	99	98	-	84	99	98	-	-	-	87	96	99	99	-	99	-	95	86
Make school interesting	76	79	80	-	71	53	56	-	-	-	70	64	63	77	-	86	-	36	58
Attract students	37	57	20	-	11	14	9	-	-	-	39	5	36	22	-	27	-	7	15
Improve achievement	64	78	74	-	70	34	45	-	-	-	66	57	58	69	-	87	-	23	76
Curric/method up-to-date	85	83	86	-	42	91	84	-	-	-	76	45	71	86	-	81	-	53	89
Individualized learning	56	71	71	-	76	38	53	-	-	-	83	50	55	56	-	57	-	52	67
Cooperative learning	44	54	39	-	51	45	75	-	-	-	53	47	26	39	-	77	-	34	48
Opportunity to acquire	46	52	59	-	62	37	67	-	-	-	80	43	49	31	-	64	-	34	39
Teachers were interested	88	85	89	-	60	68	72	-	-	-	72	72	90	85	-	82	-	81	59
Upper secondary schools																			
Experience for future	99	99	98	89	94	97	96	94	96	95	92	97	-	98	91	99	99	99	96
Make school interesting	69	78	80	38	65	48	65	57	67	89	64	44	-	62	76	84	79	40	55
Attract students	30	55	20	48	33	13	29	53	37	63	63	23	-	33	42	33	40	14	17
Improve achievement	65	83	74	44	72	24	48	65	75	75	47	56	-	79	71	84	77	35	76
Curric/method up-to-date	90	82	86	55	73	93	82	83	62	78	76	77	-	83	81	82	90	81	91
Individualized learning	51	71	71	41	74	29	56	46	57	66	59	33	-	46	61	57	66	39	66
Cooperative learning	40	56	39	18	63	35	61	38	58	47	42	20	-	37	38	78	43	31	43
Opportunity to acquire	48	46	59	58	58	34	80	70	52	31	72	52	-	37	60	66	68	24	43
Teachers were interested	95	85	89	52	78	67	80	77	62	64	66	82	-	82	58	83	74	83	71

Note. - = data not collected.

Table 3.2

Percentage of computer coordinators indicating in which context students receive most of their instruction in learning about computers

Country / Educational System

	BFL	BFR	CBC	CHI	FRA	FRG	GRE	HUN	IND	ISR	JPN	LUX	NET	NWZ	POL	POR	SLO	SWI	USA
Lower secondary schools																			
Separate course	87	90	79	-	10	81	100	-	-	-	24	93	91	67	-	35	-	90	51
Mathematics	4	0	0	-	13	10	0	-	-	-	36	0	1	8	-	19	-	6	13
Science	0	2	0	-	2	0	0	-	-	-	9	0	1	0	-	0	-	0	2
Mother tongue	0	0	7	-	2	0	0	-	-	-	0	0	1	4	-	2	-	1	6
Foreign language	2	0	0	-	1	0	0	-	-	-	1	0	0	0	-	0	-	0	0
Creative arts	0	0	0	-	0	0	0	-	-	-	0	0	0	0	-	2	-	0	0
Social studies	0	0	1	-	1	0	0	-	-	-	1	0	0	3	-	2	-	0	0
Commercial studies	0	3	0	-	1	2	0	-	-	-	0	7	1	8	-	0	-	0	4
Technology, general	4	2	11	-	54	1	0	-	-	-	29	0	0	0	-	0	-	0	-
Technology, specific	1	0	1	-	5	0	0	-	-	-	0	0	1	0	-	2	-	0	0
Home economics	0	0	1	-	1	0	0	-	-	-	0	0	0	0	-	0	-	0	0
Informal instruction	2	0	0	-	7	4	0	-	-	-	0	0	0	9	-	30	-	1	1
Upper secondary schools																			
Separate course	94	84	79	96	25	79	96	55	81	94	30	-	53	94	89	68	95	84	59
Mathematics	2	0	0	2	6	13	4	3	4	1	18	-	11	4	2	4	0	5	7
Science	0	1	0	1	2	0	0	0	11	0	5	-	0	0	0	0	0	0	2
Mother tongue	0	0	7	0	0	0	0	0	1	0	1	-	0	0	0	0	0	0	4
Foreign language	0	0	0	0	1	0	0	0	0	1	0	-	0	0	0	0	0	0	0
Creative arts	0	0	0	0	0	0	0	0	0	0	0	-	0	0	0	0	0	0	0
Social studies	0	0	1	0	0	0	0	0	0	0	0	-	0	0	0	1	0	0	0
Commercial studies	1	9	0	42	3	0	0	1	0	1	27	-	1	2	0	3	0	5	9
Technology, general	0	2	11	0	4	1	0	25	0	0	18	-	0	0	0	0	0	0	-
Technology, specific	3	3	0	0	15	0	0	1	1	3	0	-	32	0	0	9	2	4	0
Home economics	0	0	1	0	0	0	0	0	0	0	0	-	0	0	3	0	0	0	0
Informal instruction	0	0	0	1	0	3	0	7	0	0	0	-	0	0	5	9	0	0	1

Note. - = data not collected.

The use of *computers as an aid in teaching and learning* can be seen as the crucial issue of the introduction of computers in schools. Most claims about the beneficial aspects of computers are related to the integration of computers in the teaching and learning of existing subjects. This integration of computers is the most complex aspect of introducing computers in education because it requires, among other things, an extensive training of teachers and role changes related to their existing teaching practices.

A first question to address is how many teachers are using computers. For a subset of countries that handed in complete data sets, we were able to estimate the percentage of teachers in computer using schools actually using computers for instructional purposes (see Table 3.3). Although this is a rough indicator (counting even teachers that use computers marginally), it is quite interesting to see in Table 3.3 that in computer using elementary schools most of the teachers in grades 4-6 use computers. However, in lower secondary schools in most countries the integration of computers in existing subjects is still an activity of a rather small group of teachers. In upper secondary schools the percentage of teachers using computers is higher than in lower secondary schools, except for Germany (mathematics and mother tongue), New Zealand (mother tongue) and Portugal. Especially revealing, but also promising for the near future, are the relatively high percentages of computer-using teachers in the USA, where in 1989 (compared to 1985) a considerable increase of teacher use could be observed. Table 3.3 also shows that, as a trend, mathematics teachers are more inclined to use computers for their lessons than teachers in other subjects. In New Zealand there is a relatively high proportion of mother tongue teachers in lower secondary schools using computers.

Table 3.3

Percentage of teachers of existing subjects using computers in computer using schools

Country / Educational System

	BFL	FRG	IND	ISR	LUX	NET	NWZ	POL	POR	SWI	USA
Elementary schools	-	-	-	96	-	74	92	-	-	-	76
Lower secondary schools											
Mathematics	8	42	-	-	8	14	38	-	20	21	56
Science	4	10	-	-	m	4	17	-	15	15	39
Mother tongue	3	17	-	-	7	8	36	-	7	11	44
Upper secondary schools											
Mathematics	30	28	44	5	-	61	64	28	9	45	61
Science	21	22	53	6	-	32	37	11	7	31	58
Mother tongue	5	4	10	2	-	8	12	1	2	10	47

Note. - = data not collected, m = insufficient number of cases (n<50 or missing cases >20%).

Table 3.4
Percentage of computer coordinators indicating computer use in particular subjects

Country / Educational System

Subjects	BFL	BFR	CBC	CHI	FRA	FRG	GRE	HUN	IND	ISR	JPN	LUX	NET	NWZ	POL	POR	SLO	SWI	USA
Elementary schools																			
Informatics	-	79	60	-	89	-	-	-	-	39	48	-	48	72	-	35	-	-	65
Mathematics	-	75	76	-	82	-	-	-	-	86	96	-	92	78	-	54	-	-	83
Science	-	22	54	-	42	-	-	-	-	13	51	-	11	36	-	23	-	-	51
Mother tongue	-	69	90	-	84	-	-	-	-	74	55	-	94	79	-	26	-	-	79
Foreign language	-	2	4	-	1	-	-	-	-	74	0	-	16	4	-	24	-	-	4
Creative arts	-	13	44	-	40	-	-	-	-	9	21	-	27	31	-	27	-	-	13
Social studies	-	31	63	-	44	-	-	-	-	16	37	-	87	32	-	28	-	-	51
Commercial studies	-	0	43	-	0	-	-	-	-	0	0	-	0	26	-	0	-	-	0
Technology general	-	1	11	-	29	-	-	-	-	0	0	-	0	0	-	0	-	-	0
Lower secondary schools																			
Informatics	88	93	91	-	76	93	97	-	-	-	26	100	94	77	-	15	-	97	68
Mathematics	36	51	68	-	89	84	12	-	-	-	58	59	62	84	-	42	-	66	68
Science	14	15	66	-	56	39	0	-	-	-	46	37	32	25	-	19	-	41	43
Mother tongue	0	16	69	-	72	37	0	-	-	-	20	22	40	83	-	14	-	42	60
Foreign language	22	12	15	-	51	22	2	-	-	-	30	15	22	25	-	9	-	22	6
Creative arts	2	3	54	-	16	9	0	-	-	-	11	0	8	21	-	9	-	20	13
Social studies	6	5	53	-	31	30	0	-	-	-	27	11	26	54	-	21	-	18	31
Commercial studies	15	33	86	-	29	27	2	-	-	-	0	45	28	70	-	19	-	31	22
Technology general	17	5	44	-	76	12	2	-	-	-	36	4	15	0	-	2	-	6	-
Technology specific	11	13	47	-	29	10	0	-	-	-	0	19	29	18	-	10	-	7	14
Home economics	2	0	24	-	14	1	0	-	-	-	10	4	2	7	-	0	-	3	13
Upper secondary schools																			
Informatics	96	92	91	92	81	92	97	73	98	98	50	-	72	90	81	67	98	97	90
Mathematics	50	63	68	32	64	94	23	66	62	26	51	-	59	83	63	32	54	54	71
Science	35	34	66	31	54	65	3	51	64	34	43	-	42	35	57	31	35	45	58
Mother tongue	0	11	69	2	33	34	0	9	22	15	13	-	33	61	4	12	5	21	57
Foreign language	39	12	15	6	32	19	0	32	14	26	16	-	36	15	18	10	13	13	23
Creative arts	9	3	54	1	6	8	3	5	13	5	5	-	3	23	3	4	2	7	20
Social studies	8	4	54	4	21	41	4	10	19	5	17	-	33	55	2	17	8	17	32
Commercial studies	52	54	85	10	64	19	33	9	19	41	31	-	35	83	1	35	16	54	75
Technology general	16	7	44	1	34	7	3	37	4	7	15	-	0	0	0	4	7	11	-
Technology specific	25	20	47	4	48	18	6	34	9	34	0	-	18	24	2	23	22	22	43
Home economics	8	2	24	0	7	1	0	0	2	0	14	-	0	4	20	0	5	1	33

Note. - = data not collected.

For a complete overview of the subjects for which computers are used in schools (irrespective of the number of teachers using computers in a subject and, hence, different from Table 3.3) we refer to Table 3.4. This table shows that across populations in most countries the use of computers is most frequently mentioned for informatics, mathematics and science; in elementary and lower secondary schools mother tongue and social studies are mentioned relatively frequently too, while in upper secondary schools in quite some countries commercial studies are mentioned.

How teachers use computers

The results that will be presented in this section should be seen in the context of the description provided in the previous section which showed that (simply by looking at the percentage of teachers using computers in mathematics, science and mother tongue), in most countries, the integration of computers in existing subjects is not very widespread. However, even though in most countries still very few teachers use computers as an aid in their instructional practice, it is worthwhile to see for which purposes computers are used by these teachers.

Table 3.5
Medians of number of computers, number of students sharing computers, and amount of time computers are used according to teachers in existing subjects

Country / Educational System

	BFL	BFR	CBC	CHI	FRA	FRG	HUN	IND	ISR	JPN	LUX	NET	NWZ	POL	POR	SLO	SWI	USA
Elementary schools																		
# computers	-	7	14	-	6	-	-	-	16	17	-	1	1	-	-	-	-	4
# students sharing	-	2	2	-	2	-	-	-	1	2	-	2	2	-	-	-	-	1
# hours per year	-	30	35	-	25	-	-	-	60	15	-	10	20	-	-	-	-	m
Lower secondary schools																		
# computers	m	m	20	-	10	9	-	-	-	22	m	m	13	-	m	-	8	10
# students sharing	m	m	2	-	2	2	-	-	-	2	m	m	2	-	m	-	2	1
# minutes per lesson	m	m	45	-	30	m	-	-	-	30	m	m	40	-	m	-	30	28
Upper secondary schools																		
# computers	8	m	14	m	8	9	7	2	m	24	-	m	12	4	m	m	10	10
# students sharing	2	m	2	m	2	2	2	5	m	2	-	m	2	4	m	m	2	1
# minutes per lesson	30	m	30	m	30	m	20	60	m	38	-	m	40	20	m	m	21	30

Notes. - = data not collected, m = insufficient number of cases (n<50 or missing cases >20%).

Table 3.5 gives an overview of the number of computers that are available for use in existing subjects, the number of students sharing a computer and the minutes of computer use by students per lesson in which computers are used. Table 3.6 contains figures on supervision, the location of computer use and whether computers are used as whole class activities and what other students are doing if this is not the case. Table 3.7 shows the percentage of teachers using particular approaches when applying computers in their lessons. Finally, Appendix C contains Table C.1, showing the percentage of teachers using particular software. The latter table provides some insight into what teachers are doing when using computers. In future reports, more detailed information, like the curricular topics for which computers are used will be included.

Tables 3.5 - 3.7 (and Table C.1 in Appendix C) can be used to construct a global picture of how teachers of existing subjects use computers. We will give a description for each population level separately.

In many **elementary schools** in Belgium-French, Israel, and Japan computers are used as a whole class activity that very frequently takes place in a special computer room. Supervision usually takes place by the classroom teacher. In Israel and the USA 20-30% of the teachers have other teaching staff or technical aids available for supervision. In the Netherlands, New Zealand and the USA computers are apparently frequently located in the classroom and used there. The results show that the most common arrangement is to have two students share one computer and that the median number of computers varies between 1 and 16. The latter figures indicate that in Belgium-French, France, Netherlands, New Zealand, and the USA, in many schools computers cannot be used by the whole class, but that part of the students have to perform other activities while others are working at the computer.

Table 3.7 shows that computers are used for quite a range of pedagogical approaches. Self exploratory activities by students occur quite frequently in Belgium-French, New Zealand, and the USA. The content of this activity probably differs, as Table C.1 in Appendix C shows that many teachers in Belgium-French use LOGO, while in New Zealand and the USA simulation-approaches are frequently used. Tutorial approaches are especially frequently used in elementary schools in the USA and New Zealand, but not so frequently in Japan. In France and Belgium-French, large groups of students in elementary schools are tested by computer.

Table 3.6

Percentages of teachers of existing subjects indicating supervision activities, location of computer use and activities of other students

Country / Educational System

	BFL	BFR	CBC	CHI	FRA	FRG	GRE	HUN	IND	ISR	JPN	LUX	NET	NWZ	POL	POR	SLO	SWI	USA
Elementary schools																			
Supervision																			
Classroom teacher	-	66	75	-	87	-	-	-	-	60	78	-	73	72	-	-	-	-	59
Teacher & other pers	-	19	14	-	10	-	-	-	-	9	18	-	10	13	-	-	-	-	13
Other teaching staff	-	8	7	-	2	-	-	-	-	11	2	-	4	3	-	-	-	-	11
Technical aide	-	1	1	-	0	-	-	-	-	18	0	-	1	0	-	-	-	-	7
Student	-	0	1	-	1	-	-	-	-	1	1	-	3	6	-	-	-	-	2
Other supervision	-	5	4	-	1	-	-	-	-	1	0	-	9	6	-	-	-	-	8
Location																			
In normal classroom	-	32	26	-	26	-	-	-	-	5	11	-	49	83	-	-	-	-	45
Computer laboratory	-	62	63	-	57	-	-	-	-	91	82	-	10	6	-	-	-	-	45
In another place	-	6	11	-	17	-	-	-	-	4	7	-	42	12	-	-	-	-	10
Activity other students																			
All at the same time	-	48	18	-	12	-	-	-	-	42	55	-	3	3	-	-	-	-	26
Working individually	-	16	49	-	53	-	-	-	-	25	11	-	57	33	-	-	-	-	39
Have lesson/review	-	22	13	-	11	-	-	-	-	15	4	-	4	24	-	-	-	-	21
Work in small groups	-	6	5	-	19	-	-	-	-	11	13	-	18	11	-	-	-	-	7
Other activities	-	7	15	-	6	-	-	-	-	6	17	-	19	29	-	-	-	-	8
Lower secondary schools																			
Supervision																			
Classroom teacher	m	m	71	-	94	91	-	-	-	-	89	m	m	84	-	m	-	95	72
Teacher & other pers	m	m	19	-	6	6	-	-	-	-	10	m	m	10	-	m	-	2	19
Other teaching staff	m	m	5	-	0	1	-	-	-	-	1	m	m	2	-	m	-	3	6
Technical aide	m	m	2	-	0	0	-	-	-	-	0	m	m	0	-	m	-	0	1
Student	m	m	0	-	0	1	-	-	-	-	0	m	m	1	-	m	-	0	1
Other supervision	m	m	3	-	0	0	-	-	-	-	0	m	m	3	-	m	-	0	1
Location																			
In normal classroom	m	m	16	-	5	3	-	-	-	-	3	m	m	5	-	m	-	25	39
Computer laboratory	m	m	79	-	93	95	-	-	-	-	87	m	m	86	-	m	-	69	55
In another place	m	m	5	-	2	1	-	-	-	-	11	m	m	10	-	m	-	6	6
Activity other students																			
All at the same time	m	m	56	-	55	82	-	-	-	-	64	m	m	62	-	m	-	37	44
Working individually	m	m	31	-	24	6	-	-	-	-	4	m	m	19	-	m	-	44	29
Have lesson/review	m	m	1	-	5	4	-	-	-	-	2	m	m	3	-	m	-	3	11
Work in small groups	m	m	4	-	13	4	-	-	-	-	12	m	m	4	-	m	-	14	10
Other activities	m	m	8	-	4	4	-	-	-	-	18	m	m	12	-	m	-	2	6
Upper secondary schools																			
Supervision																			
Classroom teacher	88	97	83	m	95	95	-	82	52	m	83	-	m	94	64	m	m	88	82
Teacher & other pers	4	0	6	m	4	3	-	8	41	m	15	-	m	1	23	m	m	5	9
Other teaching staff	4	3	5	m	0	2	-	2	3	m	2	-	m	0	3	m	m	4	5
Technical aide	0	0	0	m	0	0	-	1	1	m	0	-	m	1	2	m	m	0	1
Student	2	0	0	m	1	0	-	6	1	m	0	-	m	1	6	m	m	0	1
Other supervision	4	0	5	m	0	0	-	1	2	m	0	-	m	2	2	m	m	4	2
Location																			
In normal classroom	30	31	31	m	16	18	-	36	3	m	3	-	m	15	61	m	m	18	51
Computer laboratory	67	54	61	m	77	82	-	54	96	m	85	-	m	79	39	m	m	73	43
In another place	4	14	8	m	7	0	-	10	1	m	12	-	m	6	0	m	m	9	6
Activity other students																			
All at the same time	62	75	42	m	66	76	-	55	23	m	65	-	m	63	49	m	m	53	39
Working individually	21	6	38	m	15	7	-	27	14	m	5	-	m	11	19	m	m	13	27
Have lesson/review	0	3	4	m	3	2	-	12	24	m	2	-	m	5	10	m	m	1	4
Work in small groups	13	9	6	m	15	8	-	7	25	m	12	-	m	4	13	m	m	21	17
Other activities	4	6	10	m	2	7	-	0	14	m	16	-	m	17	10	m	m	11	13

Notes. - = data not collected, m = insufficient number of cases (n<50 or missing cases >20%).

Table 3.7
Percentage of teachers of existing subjects using particular instructional approaches

Country / Educational System

	BFL	BFR	CBC	CHI	FRA	FRG	GRE	HUN	IND	ISR	JPN	LUX	NET	NWZ	POL	POR	SLO	SWI	USA
Elementary schools																			
Drill, practice	-	85	78	-	88	.	.	.	-	-	92	86	-	88	78	.	.	.	-	93
Instruc. by comp.	-	38	64	-	49	.	.	.	-	-	45	19	-	54	68	.	.	.	-	72
Teacher demonstrates	-	51	65	-	57	.	.	.	-	-	25	42	-	18	48	.	.	.	-	54
Students tested	-	56	16	-	62	.	.	.	-	-	20	13	-	48	19	.	.	.	-	27
Enrichment	-	46	58	-	34	.	.	.	-	-	56	32	-	38	66	.	.	.	-	68
Remediation	-	45	51	-	30	.	.	.	-	-	42	38	-	52	63	.	.	.	-	65
Students self-explore	-	52	72	-	32	.	.	.	-	-	15	34	-	32	60	.	.	.	-	56
Lower secondary schools																			
Drill, practice	m	m	48	-	94	95	.	.	.	-	78	m	m	62	-	m	-	64	75
Instruc. by comp.	m	m	46	-	45	56	.	.	.	-	27	m	m	59	-	m	-	35	55
Teacher demonstrates	m	m	56	-	38	77	.	.	.	-	54	m	m	46	-	m	-	63	44
Students tested	m	m	11	-	69	17	.	.	.	-	13	m	m	14	-	m	-	15	26
Enrichment	m	m	29	-	46	39	.	.	.	-	16	m	m	30	-	m	-	46	59
Remediation	m	m	23	-	48	0	.	.	.	-	24	m	m	33	-	m	-	26	55
Students self-explore	m	m	49	-	25	26	.	.	.	-	26	m	m	51	-	m	-	36	50
Upper secondary schools																			
Drill, practice	46	75	44	m	83	78	-	39	79	m	49	-	m	44	66	m	m	44	44
Instruc. by comp.	18	19	39	m	35	31	-	24	77	50	36	-	m	49	75	m	m	22	52
Teacher demonstrates	49	56	47	m	36	84	-	72	83	56	59	-	m	49	75	m	m	73	62
Students tested	14	22	20	m	47	6	-	26	53	25	14	-	m	10	33	m	m	17	16
Enrichment	9	25	31	m	26	18	-	39	55	25	14	-	m	21	36	m	m	37	50
Remediation	7	17	28	m	25	0	-	19	49	25	11	-	m	11	25	m	m	18	33
Students self-explore	23	28	57	m	28	46	-	61	52	50	36	-	m	44	41	m	m	49	45

Notes. - = data not collected, m = insufficient number of cases (n<50 or missing cases >20%).

This may look surprising, as the computer coordinators in Belgium-French, and France don't report the availability of software for testing like item banks and scoring. An explanation for this phenomenon (such as, for example, facilities for testing in drill and practice programs) will be sought in future analyses.

In **lower secondary schools**, computers are used most frequently in special computer rooms. The USA has the highest percentage (39%) of teachers who can use computers in their classrooms. In a few countries, computer use is organized largely as a whole class activity, but in most other countries large groups of teachers have to organize separate activities for the students not using computers. The problems resulting from this organizational set-up may be related to problems teachers experience in using computers (see, for instance, 'preparation time for lessons' and 'difficulties with the organization of lessons' in Table 3.8). Similar to elementary schools we find that in lower secondary schools drill and practice is the most frequently mentioned approach. However, it should be noted that about half of the teachers in British Columbia, New Zealand, Portugal, and the USA report that students are involved in self exploratory activities. Again, as in elementary education the content of these activities may differ. This will be explored in future analyses.

In **upper secondary schools** computers are more often used in the classroom (compared to elementary and lower secondary education), while it is also more common to organize computer use as a whole class activity. Also, teacher demonstration and self exploration are mentioned more frequently at this level than at the lower levels of education. One may also observe that the use of programming languages is frequently mentioned by teachers at this level.

From a comparison of Table 3.5 with Table 2.2 (the number of computers in schools according to computer coordinators), some anomalies seem to arise. Most noteworthy is that the computer coordinators in Japan indicated that the median number of available computers is 7, whereas the teachers in existing subjects report to have a median of 22 computers available for their lessons. Further inspection of the data for Japan revealed that there is not an inconsistency between computer coordinators and teachers, but rather that those teachers who use computers in existing subjects come from schools, where on the average, about 24 computers are available.

Another interesting finding in Table 3.5 is that, in general, the number of students sharing a computer is quite stable despite large variations in the available number of computers. Figure 3.1 illustrates why this might be the case. In this Figure a distinction is made between four different organizational set-ups, namely computer use (1) in the classroom by a part of the students, (2) in the classroom by all students at the same time, (3) outside the classroom by part of the students, and (4) outside the classroom by all students at the same time. For each of these set-ups and each population, the Figure shows the average number of students sharing computers and the average number of computers available. First, the percentages below the figure show that, when combining the samples of teachers from across all countries, the use of computers as a whole-class activity in the classroom is quite low and that, in such a situation, a relatively large number of students have to share computers. For the other situations (whole-class-outside classroom; part-class-in-classroom and part-class-outside classroom), the number of students sharing computers is quite stable. However, the number of computers available for each situation differs considerably, showing that whole class activities take place if the number of computers is about 20. So, it seems that the typical computer useing teacher in existing subjects strives for a student:computer ratio of 2:1 during the lessons, which means that in case there are not enough computers, classes are split up.

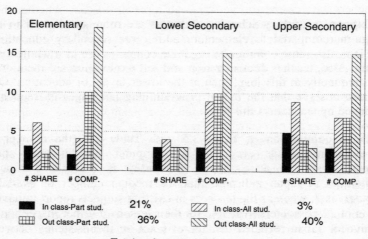

Figure 3.1 Number of computers, number of students sharing a computer and organization of class in elementary, lower secondary schools and upper secondary schools.

Changes perceived by teachers as a result of using computers

As indicated in the first chapter, stage 1 of this study did not include any student measures. Hence, the effect of using computers could not be studied during this stage of the project. Nevertheless, the question of what teachers see as effects of using computers is interesting, because teachers' positive or negative perceptions may influence their own future use of computers in the classroom as well as that of their colleagues who still are not using computers. On the other hand the teacher perceptions used in this study might also reflect real effects, although at this moment the possibility that the perceptions reflect attitudes instead of real effects cannot be ruled out. In order to find out whether teachers observed any changes as a result of using computers in their lessons the following list of possible changes was presented: (1) curriculum content covered; (2) time students spent working individually; (3) time spent in small-group work; (4) time spent in whole-class activities; (5) interest of students in this subject; (6) preparation time for lessons; (7) students achievement in this subject; (8) availability of feedback about student achievement; (9) difficulty in organizing lesson AND (10) students tutoring and helping each other.

Teachers were asked to rate, for each topic in this list, whether they had observed a large decrease, slight decrease, no change, slight increase or large increase. After having combined the categories "slight increase" and "large increase" we calculated for each topic in the list the percentage of teachers choosing one of these response alternatives. The results are included in Table 3.8.

Table 3.8 shows that in many countries teachers frequently reported that the interest of students increased as a result of using computers. Moreover, a large percentage of teachers (for instance in elementary schools in Belgium-French, British Columbia, France and New Zealand) seem to have observed increases in student achievement. It is also clear that (according to the perceptions of teachers), students are more engaged in cooperative and individual work, whereas the time spent on whole-class activities, in general, decreases. The question whether by using computers more curriculum content can be covered does not get an unequivocal answer. The percentage of teachers observing increases in this area is relatively low, although some remarkably high figures are found in some countries (for instance in elementary schools in New Zealand). In some countries (elementary schools in the Netherlands, lower secondary schools in Belgium-Flemish, Belgium-France, Japan and the Netherlands), teachers report an increased difficulty in organizing lessons. Furthermore, especially in lower and upper secondary education, the time needed for preparing lessons increases.

Problems teachers encounter in using computers and reasons for not using computers

As indicated in Chapter I, the introduction of computers in education is a complex innovation that can only be implemented successfully if a large number of conditions are fulfilled.

Table 3.8
Percentage of teachers of existing subjects perceiving small or large changes as a result of using computers

Country / Educational System

Type of Change	BFL	BFR	CBC	CHI	FRA	FRG	GRE	HUN	IND	ISR	JPN	LUX	NET	NWZ	POL	POR	SLO	SWI	USA
Elementary schools																			
Content covered	-	16	20	-	12	-	-	-	-	37	15	-	27	63	-	-	-	-	32
Time indiv. work	-	57	51	-	48	-	-	-	-	68	56	-	36	56	-	-	-	-	30
Time small-group	-	63	39	-	58	-	-	-	-	33	35	-	13	57	-	-	-	-	25
Time whole-class	-	15	13	-	6	-	-	-	-	10	13	-	3	11	-	-	-	-	9
Interest students	-	91	85	-	77	-	-	-	-	74	85	-	39	93	-	-	-	-	65
Prepar. time lessons	-	38	32	-	40	-	-	-	-	11	63	-	41	35	-	-	-	-	28
Students achievem.	-	63	67	-	66	-	-	-	-	58	44	-	30	79	-	-	-	-	58
Avail.feedb.achievement	-	32	34	-	14	-	-	-	-	51	31	-	27	54	-	-	-	-	65
Diffic.organiz. lesson	-	41	32	-	33	-	-	-	-	6	44	-	61	40	-	-	-	-	18
Students help each other	-	81	80	-	75	-	-	-	-	60	63	-	46	92	-	-	-	-	55
Lower secondary schools																			
Content covered	m	m	20	-	9	15	-	-	-	-	11	m	m	34	-	m	-	10	20
Time indiv. work	m	m	56	-	59	56	-	-	-	-	56	m	m	43	-	m	-	12	36
Time small-group	m	m	39	-	52	57	-	-	-	-	36	m	m	49	-	m	-	45	35
Time whole-class	m	m	9	-	8	14	-	-	-	-	5	m	m	10	-	m	-	41	10
Interest students	m	m	84	-	81	74	-	-	-	-	74	m	m	83	-	m	-	88	61
Prepar. time lessons	m	m	33	-	47	79	-	-	-	-	74	m	m	36	-	m	-	74	36
Students achievem.	m	m	64	-	54	38	-	-	-	-	27	m	m	58	-	m	-	49	52
Avail.feedb.achievement	m	m	38	-	26	22	-	-	-	-	25	m	m	35	-	m	-	38	69
Diffic.organiz. lesson	m	m	30	-	39	49	-	-	-	-	54	m	m	43	-	m	-	40	20
Students help each other	m	m	80	-	75	61	-	-	-	-	66	m	m	78	-	m	-	76	55
Upper secondary schools																			
Content covered	33	8	25	m	5	18	-	41	40	m	17	-	m	27	26	m	m	8	23
Time indiv. work	31	27	63	m	43	50	-	38	55	m	40	-	m	41	44	m	m	11	40
Time small-group	37	43	37	m	53	58	-	43	57	m	28	-	m	52	38	m	m	31	36
Time whole-class	8	16	20	m	6	24	-	23	45	m	11	-	m	8	21	m	m	39	12
Interest students	67	76	71	m	73	56	-	82	87	m	82	-	m	71	72	m	m	64	54
Prepar. time lessons	69	78	42	m	55	73	-	70	46	m	68	-	m	52	51	m	m	73	41
Students achievem.	35	46	57	m	41	18	-	41	76	m	29	-	m	44	36	m	m	34	53
Avail.feedb.achievement	10	24	39	m	21	14	-	33	47	m	28	-	m	30	36	m	m	27	68
Diffic.organiz. lesson	48	57	39	m	40	47	-	70	31	m	36	-	m	49	43	m	m	37	18
Students help each other	73	62	76	m	72	53	-	63	63	m	62	-	m	73	39	m	m	66	54

Notes. - = data not collected, m = insufficient number of cases (n<50 or missing cases >20%).

The picture emerging from the previous sections is that the integration of computers in the curriculum is very gradually developing, but it is especially promising to see that, for instance in the USA, in a 4-year period twice as many teachers are using computers in their lessons (Becker, 1990) In other countries, however, the implementation of computers seems to be in a much earlier stage than the USA.

In order to find out what teachers (who use computers as well as the non users) see as the major obstacles in using computers one may look at the problems users experience as well as the reasons for not using computers as indicated by the non using teachers. Such an exploration might identify those areas where policy makers and support institutes might take measures for improving the conditions for optimizing the implementation process.

Tables D.7, D.10 and D.11 (in Appendix D) contain the percentages of teachers that cited a particular problem in using computers in their selection of the five most serious problems from a list of 28. These tables show that the four problems that are most frequently mentioned are: lack of hardware, lack of software, problems with finding enough time to learn about computers or to prepare lessons in which computers are used. In elementary schools, teachers also frequently mention their lack of knowledge. The ranking of these problems in terms of relative frequencies differ from country to country and future analyses should be aimed at trying to identify which circumstances are of potential influence on what teachers perceive as problems in using computers.

What do the results show?

Most notable is that in many countries only a small percentage of teachers in secondary schools are using computers. An exception is the USA where almost half of the teachers in secondary schools use computers in their lessons. Generally, teachers organize the use computers in such a way that 2-3 students share the available equipment and, if necessary, the class is split up allowing one group to work with computers, while the other students perform other activities. Drill and practice is very frequently mentioned as an approach for which computers are used. Many teachers experience a lack of software and time constraints as the most serious problems in using computers in schools.

References

Becker, H. J. (1990). *Computer use in the United States schools: 1989. An initial report of U.S. participation in the I.E.A. Computers in Education Survey.* Paper presented at the 1990 meetings of the American Educational Research Association.

Chapter IV
Staff Development

Staff development is considered to be an important issue when dealing with the implementation of an innovation. This chapter contains a description of the status of staff development in all educational systems: who supports the activities, what topics are dealt with and what informal training activities take place. As the past experience of teachers is an important conditional factor, a description of this characteristic of teachers is given as well as their opinion about their knowledge and skills.
The results show that staff development activities mainly include introductory and application courses and in secondary schools also programming courses. The knowledge and skills of computer education teachers in general outreaches that of other teachers, whereas using teachers of existing subjects know more than their non using colleagues.

Introduction

In the introduction of educational changes in general, and certainly also in the implementation of computers in education, it constantly turns out that the teacher is the central factor in the failure or success of the innovation (Van den Akker, Keursten & Plomp, in press; Office of Technology Assessment, 1988). Usually, the teacher decides whether or not he or she will use the computer in the teaching-learning process, and determines how it will be used. Teachers need to be trained in order to be knowledgeable in the use of computers. The previous chapter showed that a lack of knowledge is seen as one of the major problems in using computers as well as the major reason for not using computers in schools. Hence, the question arises what staff development facilities are available for teachers and how staff development is organized. Staff development is supposed to be an important aspect of a policy (at all levels) directed at introducing new technologies in the schools. Such a policy on national, state, local or school level should not be restricted to just providing some in-service training opportunities. It should rather address the major factors influencing the introduction of computers in education, as outlined in Chapter I.

In this chapter, a description will be given of the availability of facilities for staff development. First some context data will be presented, namely a summary of national or state policies on staff development, and background data of computer using teachers. Then the availability, the content and the providers of teacher training will be described. We will look at informal staff development activities in order to get an indication whether training is just a one-shot activity, or followed up by activities in the schools. Next the status of the knowledge and skills of teachers (as measured by their self-ratings of knowledge and skills) will be discussed, which can be considered as the results of staff development activities. Finally, we will present some opinions on and problems related to teacher training.

Summary of national or state policies

By means of a national questionnaire, data were collected regarding the policies on pre-service and in-service teacher training in computers in each participating educational system. These national questionnaires showed that in most educational systems educational authorities support (pre-service as well as in-service) teacher training. Only Hungary reported no direct involvement of authorities. In educational systems with a clearly decentral system, like the USA and Switzerland, this support is provided by state or regional authorities (school districts, cantons). Authority support consists predominantly of providing facilities to teacher training colleges or other agencies in charge with teacher (in-service) training.

In order to characterize policies with respect to teacher training on the use of computers in education, each participating national center was asked to check the appropriate categories from the following list:
- the government considers it its task to train all teachers (*task government*);
- a certain number of teachers should be trained and should train others (*cascade model*);
- schools should arrange and pay for their teachers to attend commercially available teacher training courses (*schools' responsibility*);
- teachers interested in the use of computers should find their own ways of getting trained and at their own expenses (*teachers' responsibility*);
- all teachers graduating at present have had a training during their initial teacher training (*initial training*);
- all teachers are offered (in-service) training on three levels, either user

level, advanced user level, or programmer level (*opportunity for all*). The results are summarized in Table 4.1.

Table 4.1
Characterization of policies on teacher training per population (indicated by the National Project Coordinator)

Country / educational System

	BFL	BFR	FRA	GRE	HUN	IND	ITA	LUX	NET	NWZ	POL	POR	SWI	USA	N*
Task government	1/2/3	?	1/2/3	-	-	3	-	1/2/3	2/3	-	-	-	2/3[c]	1/2/3[d]	(7)
Cascade model	-	1/2/3	1/2/3	2/3	1/2/3	-	2/3	-	2	1/2/3	-	1/2/3	2/3[c]	1/2/3[e]	(10)
Schools' responsibility	-	-	-	-	1/2/3	-	1/2/3	-	-	-	-	-	2/3[c]	-	(3)
Teachers' responsibility	-	1/2/3	-	-	1/2/3	-	1/2	-	-	1/2/3	-	-	-	1/2/3[d]	(5)
Initial training	-	?	-	2/3	-	-	-	1/2/3	-	1/2/3[b]	-	-	2/3	-	(4)
Opportunity for all	-	1/2/3[a]	-	-	1/2/3	-	-	2/3	2/3	-	2/3	-	2/3	-	(6)

Notes. * = number of countries that indicated this policy, [a] = certain teachers only, [b] = most teachers, [c] = situation differs per canton, [d] = policy on local level, [e] = policy on local and state level.

From Table 4.1 we conclude that in many educational systems (10 out of 15) a cascade model is applied for in-service training. This means that a small number of teachers is trained who are expected to train other teachers in the school. Future analyses should be aimed at investigating the effectiveness of this strategy. One might be further surprised by the relatively large number of educational systems where the training of teachers in using computers is not yet part of the initial training, and where a full package of training courses is not offered to the teachers.

Experience of teachers with computers

Staff development is considered to be an important element in introducing any innovation in schools, so also for computers in education. The experience of teachers is frequently mentioned as an important conditional factor. Experience can be expressed in terms of years of experience with computers, the number of years of using a computer for educational purposes, as well as in the use of computers at home. We will summarize the results on these variables.

Duration of computer experience

Table 4.2 shows the median of the **first year of computer use** by using as well as non using teachers.

Table 4.2
Teachers' year of first use of computers (median)

Country / Educational System

	BFL	BFR	CBC	CHI	FRA	FRG	GRE	HUN	IND	ISR	JPN	LUX	NET	NWZ	POL	POR	SLO	SWI	USA
Elementary schools																			
Non using teachers	-	85	m	-	m	-	-	-	-	m	81	-	m	m	-	-	-	-	84
Using teachers	-	84	83	-	m	-	-	-	-	85	86	-	85	86	-	-	-	-	84
Lower secondary schools																			
Computer teachers	85	m	m	-	-	84	83	-	-	-	83	82	83	80	-	m	-	83	81
Non using teachers*	85	m	82	-	84	86	m	-	-	-	83	84	84	83	-	m	-	85	83
Using teachers*	m	m	83	-	83	84	m	-	-	-	84	m	m	83	-	m	-	84	82
Upper secondary schools																			
Computer teachers	80	80	77	84	81	78	82	82	86	81	78	-	m	78	83	82	m	77	79
Non using teachers*	83	80	81	m	83	84	85	84	86	84	82	-	85	82	86	m	m	83	82
Using teachers*	82	m	82	m	82	78	m	82	86	m	82	-	m	80	m	m	m	76	80

Notes. - = data not collected, m = insufficient number of cases (n<50 or missing cases >20%),
* = (non)using teachers are teachers of existing subjects who do (not) use computers

There are quite a few educational systems where the median of the year of first computer use of teachers is in the late seventies or the early eighties. In British Columbia, New Zealand and the USA all the medians for teachers (users as well as non users) in lower and upper secondary schools and for instance Switzerland in upper secondary schools are not later than 1983. Probably the teachers in these educational systems gained their first computer experience already as students in universities and teacher training colleges. The data in Table 4.3 contains more details about the location of first computer use.

When comparing data from different educational levels, it appears that the higher the level, the earlier the first year of experience with computers. This holds for computer education teachers, as well as for teachers in mathematics, science and mother tongue. A further inspection of the data showed that within the sample of teachers in existing subjects (mathematics, science and mother tongue), mathematics teachers generally have the most experience, and mother tongue teachers the least experience with computers.

Table 4.3
Location of first computer use by teachers who ever used a computer (percentages)

Country / Educational System

	BFL	BFR	CBC	CHI	FRA	FRG	GRE	HUN	IND	ISR	JPN	LUX	NET	NWZ	POL	POR	SLO	SWI	USA
Elementary schools																			
Non using teachers*	-	57	m	-	m	-	-	-	-	m	m	-	m	82	-	-	-	-	90
At school (student)	-	m	m	-	m	-	-	-	-	m	m	-	m	m	-	-	-	-	36
At school (teacher)	-	m	m	-	m	-	-	-	-	m	m	-	m	m	-	-	-	-	30
At home	-	m	m	-	m	-	-	-	-	m	m	-	m	m	-	-	-	-	16
Elsewhere	-	m	m	-	m	-	-	-	-	m	m	-	m	m	-	-	-	-	18
Using teachers*																			
At school (student)	-	11	22	-	19	-	-	-	-	37	15	-	8	23	-	-	-	-	31
At school (teacher)	-	35	55	-	49	-	-	-	-	48	60	-	60	41	-	-	-	-	45
At home	-	31	12	-	14	-	-	-	-	7	18	-	15	18	-	-	-	-	13
Elsewhere	-	23	11	-	19	-	-	-	-	8	6	-	17	18	-	-	-	-	10
Lower secondary schools																			
Computer teachers																			
At school (student)	23	22	m	-	-	m	33	-	-	-	37	46	37	29	-	30	-	31	45
At school (teacher)	36	12	m	-	-	m	2	-	-	-	34	29	33	23	-	26	-	16	29
At home	21	36	m	-	-	m	24	-	-	-	23	22	17	20	-	17	-	30	13
Elsewhere	20	30	m	-	-	m	41	-	-	-	5	3	13	28	-	27	-	23	13
Non using teachers*	51	55	97	-	90	68	31	-	-	-	m	77	83	95	-	76	-	90	87
At school (student)	10	11	32	-	25	21	29	-	-	-	m	26	33	26	-	36	-	40	41
At school (teacher)	25	19	36	-	35	32	1	-	-	-	m	18	25	23	-	19	-	24	27
At home	32	39	14	-	15	36	30	-	-	-	m	34	21	17	-	19	-	18	16
Elsewhere	34	31	18	-	25	11	41	-	-	-	m	23	20	35	-	27	-	18	15
Using teachers*																			
At school (student)	m	m	27	-	23	21	m	-	-	-	37	m	m	24	-	m	-	25	35
At school (teacher)	m	m	43	-	48	43	m	-	-	-	37	m	m	34	-	m	-	23	46
At home	m	m	18	-	16	28	m	-	-	-	19	m	m	15	-	m	-	30	8
Elsewhere	m	m	13	-	13	8	m	-	-	-	6	m	m	26	-	m	-	22	11
Upper secondary schools																			
Computer teachers																			
At school (student)	46	49	43	56	35	51	37	47	53	58	32	-	m	27	53	33	m	51	55
At school (teacher)	19	13	22	36	42	23	0	33	21	3	40	-	m	15	19	10	m	17	24
At home	16	16	10	0	9	17	17	8	2	9	8	-	m	11	9	22	m	11	5
Elsewhere	20	22	25	7	14	9	46	12	23	29	20	-	m	47	19	35	m	20	16
Non using teachers*	82	76	99	m	87	83	42	63	38	76	m	-	88	95	76	65	74	93	89
At school (student)	24	39	39	m	19	32	25	30	46	34	m	-	28	31	34	18	37	44	46
At school (teacher)	20	6	38	m	31	37	2	32	29	5	m	-	28	27	32	20	24	27	28
At home	27	21	12	m	20	25	41	19	6	12	m	-	26	20	19	30	20	10	10
Elsewhere	30	34	12	m	30	5	32	18	20	49	m	-	18	22	15	32	19	19	15
Using teachers*																			
At school (student)	20	m	30	m	19	m	m	43	57	m	36	-	m	26	26	m	m	51	34
At school (teacher)	50	m	36	m	43	m	m	40	30	m	42	-	m	36	60	m	m	18	40
At home	11	m	21	m	23	m	m	8	1	m	14	-	m	8	11	m	m	10	14
Elsewhere	20	m	14	m	14	m	m	9	13	m	7	-	m	30	3	m	m	22	12

Notes. - = data not collected, m = insufficient number of cases (n<50 or missing cases >20%),
* = (non)using teachers are teachers of existing subjects who do (not) use computers. The first line for the category non using teachers contains the percentages of the total group of non using teachers that ever used a computer.

Table 4.3 shows **where** teachers got their first experience with computers. Across populations, the two most important locations are "at school, college or university when being a student", and "at school as a teacher".

For elementary schools, in all educational systems the most mentioned location where using teachers got their first experience with computers, is "at school as a teacher". In lower secondary schools, computer education teachers, mention most frequently "when being a student", while for upper secondary schools it holds even stronger that teachers of computer education had their first computer experience before they became a teacher. The picture is not very clear for teachers of existing subjects.

Whereas Table 4.2 showed the first year that teachers used computers at all, Table 4.4 shows how many **years teachers are already using computers** in their teaching and therefore, only computer using teachers are included here.

Table 4.4
Number of years of computer use in teaching (median)

Country / Educational System

	BFL	BFR	CBC	CHI	FRA	FRG	GRE	HUN	IND	ISR	JPN	LUX	NET	NWZ	POL	POR	SLO	SWI	USA
Elementary schools																			
Using teachers	-	3	4	-	3	-	-	-	-	3	2	-	2	2	-	-	-	-	3
Lower secondary schools																			
Computer teachers	3	3	m	-	-	3	2	-	-	-	2	3	4	3	-	2	-	3	m
Using teachers*	m	m	2	-	4	2	m	-	-	-	2	m	m	3	-	m	-	2	3
Upper secondary schools																			
Computer teachers	5	6	7	3	4	6	3	4	3	5	4	-	m	4	3	2	m	4	m
Using teachers*	4	m	4	m	4	5	m	4	3	m	2	-	m	4	3	m	m	4	3

Notes. - = data not collected, m = insufficient number of cases (n<50 or missing cases >20%),
* = using teachers are teachers of existing subjects who use computers.

Generally, upper secondary school teachers have been using computers in their teaching for the longest time, followed by teachers in lower secondary schools and then elementary schools, although the differences between the last two are not large. This finding is consistent with the results in Table 2.2, which indicates the first year of computer use at school.

In summary, at the time of data collection in 1989, teachers typically had only a few years of experience using computers for instructional purposes, although their first experience with computers at all took place earlier. Many teachers, especially in lower and upper secondary schools, got their first experience with computers before they became a teacher, during their teacher training or even before.

Use of computers at home

Teachers were asked whether they had access to a computer at home and, if so, to indicate roughly how many hours per week they used this computer. For the latter variable they could select an interval (1-5; 6-10; 11-15;16-20; or more than 20 hours); by taking the middle of the intervals (and 23 hours for the last alternative) a rough estimate for computer use at home could be calculated. Table 4.5 shows the results on these variables.

In lower and upper secondary schools in most educational systems, a vast majority of computer using teachers have access to a computer at home. In most systems no striking differences appear between percentages of computer education teachers and computer using teachers in existing subjects who do have access to computers at home. Remarkable is the high percentage of computer owners in Hungary and Poland if we take into account these educational systems' economic situation. On the other hand, the pattern found in India is more according to expectations based on socio-economic circumstances. Elementary school teachers have least access to computers at home; those who have access, spend less time on the computer at home than teachers at the other levels. In Table 4.5 we see that the percentage of using teachers having a computer at home, in general, is much higher than of non using teachers.

In most countries, in lower and upper secondary schools, computer education teachers spend slightly more hours at the computer at home than their colleagues in existing subjects, while in most countries the average number of hours for both groups varies between 5 and 10 hours per week.

The Use of Computers in Education Worldwide

Table 4.5

Percentage of computer use of teachers at home and mean number of hours of use at home

Country / Educational System

	BFL	BFR	CBC	CHI	FRA	FRG	GRE	HUN	IND	ISR	JPN	LUX	NET	NWZ	POL	POR	SLO	SWI	USA
Elementary schools																			
Non using teachers																			
Access at home	-	21	m	-	m	-	-	-	-	m	m	-	m	23	-	-	-	-	26
Mean hours per week	-	4.7	m	-	m	-	-	-	-	m	m	-	m	5.1	-	-	-	-	4.4
Using teachers																			
Access at home	-	53	56	-	26	-	-	-	-	23	m	-	41	53	-	-	-	-	40
Mean hours per week	-	4.5	5.3	-	4.7	-	-	-	-	3.7	m	-	5.1	4.2	-	-	-	-	4.9
Lower secondary schools																			
Computer teachers																			
Access at home	61	74	m	-	-	80	85	-	-	-	m	86	79	81	-	m	-	78	69
Mean hours per week	7.9	8.1	m	-	-	9.6	13.4	-	-	-	m	8.4	7.7	9.2	-	m	-	8.7	6.7
Non using teachers*																			
Access at home	26	25	54	-	29	46	17	-	-	-	m	40	55	47	-	30	-	43	43
Mean hours per week	5.8	5.8	5.9	-	5.0	6.9	6.8	-	-	-	m	4.3	5.8	4.4	-	5.4	-	5.9	5.1
Using teachers*																			
Access at home	m	m	54	-	55	83	m	-	-	-	m	m	m	69	-	m	-	75	54
Mean hours per week	m	m	6.8	-	6.6	8.0	m	-	-	-	m	m	m	5.6	-	m	-	7.5	5.7
Upper secondary schools																			
Computer teachers																			
Access at home	78	77	89	10	60	91	84	99	2	68	m	-	m	81	63	74	m	73	71
Mean hours per week	8.7	10.0	9.6	6.8	7.8	9.7	13.5	8.0	6.3	9.8	m	-	m	8.5	6.7	13.4	m	8.9	7.5
Non using teachers*																			
Access at home	48	37	55	m	38	59	20	36	m	33	m	-	59	53	32	26	m	48	43
Mean hours per week	5.2	5.5	6.0	m	5.7	6.8	7.6	4.9	m	5.9	m	-	4.9	4.5	4.7	6.8	m	6.5	5.5
Using teachers*																			
Access at home	67	m	78	m	57	83	m	56	1	m	m	-	m	70	40	m	m	76	64
Mean hours per week	8.9	m	7.9	m	6.8	9.9	m	5.7	10.5	m	m	-	m	5.3	5.4	m	m	7.9	6.2

Notes. - = data not collected, m = insufficient number of cases for the variable 'access' (n<50 or missing cases >20%),

* = (non)using teachers are teachers of existing subjects who do (not) use computers

In general, the data discussed so far illustrate that, except for India and to a lesser extent for Poland and Portugal, a majority of computer using teachers are actively working with computers at home. Moreover, the previous section showed that the typical teacher has about 3-4 years experience with using computers for instructional purposes. Still, these experiences have not led to an acceptable level of knowledge and skills in applying computers in education (see also Chapter III and Appendix D). We believe that systematic and continuous staff development is a major factor in promoting the skills of teachers. Hence, we will describe in the next section which staff development is available, by which means it is provided and what content is included.

Availability of staff development

The computer coordinators of the schools participating in the study indicated which of the following kinds of staff development were readily available for the teachers in their schools and through what agencies support is given for training:
- introductory course: how to use computers;
- using computer application programs (word processors, spreadsheets etc.);
- computer science course, programming;
- micro-electronics;
- computer science course for technical subjects (not in elementary schools);
- using computers in specific subjects.
The results are summarized in Table 4.6.

In elementary schools, the most frequently available form of staff development is an introductory course (British Columbia reports even 100%), with an application course as the second frequently mentioned; staff development in micro-electronics is hardly available.

Lower and upper secondary schools demonstrate generally similar patterns. Next to frequent availability of introductory and application courses, courses in computer science/programming and in computer use in specific subjects appear frequently, although the latter two show great variation between educational systems. Where a decade ago in many industrialized educational systems the emphasis in computer use was on programming, we now see that, although in every country still a very high percentage of computer science/programming courses is mentioned, introductory and application courses are more frequently included in teacher training in almost all educational systems compared to the number of programming courses. The high percentages on computer science for technical subjects in a few educational systems reflects the vocational schools in the sample (see also Appendix B).

The Use of Computers in Education Worldwide

Table 4.6
Availability of staff development and agency giving support (in percentages) as indicated by computer coordinators

Country / Educational System

	BFL	BFR	CBC	CHI	FRA	FRG	GRE	HUN	IND	ISR	JPN	LUX	NET	NWZ	POL	POR	SLO	SWI	USA
Elementary schools																			
Types of staff development																			
Introductory course	-	70	100	-	72	-	-	-	-	77	99	-	89	84	-	73	-	-	m
Use application programs	-	67	99	-	64	-	-	-	-	56	89	-	73	79	-	74	-	-	m
Comp.science course	-	59	57	-	62	-	-	-	-	29	19	-	51	28	-	22	-	-	m
Micro-electronics	-	13	25	-	23	-	-	-	-	3	10	-	4	12	-	2	-	-	m
Specific subjects	-	45	73	-	50	-	-	-	-	54	53	-	44	60	-	37	-	-	m
Agency																			
School	-	27	33	-	18	-	-	-	-	38	38	-	26	55	-	51	-	-	m
Local educ. authority	-	33	49	-	58	-	-	-	-	24	41	-	18	0	-	2	-	-	m
Other external agencies	-	41	18	-	24	-	-	-	-	38	20	-	56	45	-	47	-	-	m
Lower secondary schools																			
Types of staff development																			
Introductory course	80	54	90	-	87	96	75	-	-	-	m	100	90	82	-	56	-	98	80
Use application programs	81	52	91	-	84	87	63	-	-	-	m	100	83	88	-	52	-	97	75
Comp.science course	86	47	57	-	67	91	58	-	-	-	m	74	63	48	-	21	-	84	66
Micro-electronics	22	15	30	-	30	44	3	-	-	-	m	37	11	15	-	4	-	32	39
Technical subject	33	22	42	-	55	0	3	-	-	-	m	33	24	19	-	11	-	31	0
Specific subjects	35	31	75	-	76	72	13	-	-	-	m	45	55	72	-	32	-	49	60
Agency																			
School	34	24	31	-	30	24	13	-	-	-	29	26	42	73	-	68	-	28	m
Local educ. authority	28	33	32	-	41	59	27	-	-	-	51	55	13	1	-	1	-	50	m
Other external agencies	38	43	37	-	29	17	60	-	-	-	20	19	44	26	-	32	-	23	m
Upper secondary schools																			
Types of staff development																			
Introductory course	90	63	89	62	80	92	m	94	86	46	89	-	90	82	85	54	m	95	m
Use application programs	94	65	92	44	90	84	m	79	74	58	75	-	92	83	57	53	m	97	m
Comp.science course	81	59	56	45	66	94	m	80	59	37	35	-	66	45	87	19	m	89	m
Micro-electronics	19	19	30	10	29	47	m	42	23	17	25	-	21	26	19	5	m	44	m
Technical subject	36	33	42	16	65	0	m	63	26	30	27	-	22	28	24	13	m	40	m
Specific subjects	55	45	75	12	70	80	m	63	39	39	51	-	56	62	41	33	m	65	m
Agency																			
School	36	27	30	24	32	23	m	28	29	35	20	-	43	62	16	64	m	36	m
Local educ. authority	22	28	32	63	45	61	m	35	18	29	55	-	16	1	74	0	m	31	m
Other external agencies	42	46	37	13	23	16	m	37	53	36	25	-	42	37	10	36	m	33	m

Notes. - = data not collected, m = insufficient number of cases (n<50 or missing cases >20%).

Providers of training

Teacher in-service training in the new area of computers in education cannot completely be provided by the schools themselves. Support to schools may come from local (regional) educational authorities, as well as from external agencies. A first impression of the sources of support can be obtained from Table 4.6. Given the kinds of staff developments available for schools, computer coordinators were asked to indicate through what agency each kind of staff development was available; the data are aggregated over the different kinds of training. Coordinators could also indicate combinations of two or three agencies supporting staff development activities. For Table 4.6 the frequency of checking each seperate agency is determined and divided by the total number of agencies checked. Some general trends can be observed at all three educational levels. Where, in general, all three agencies play a meaningful role in offering in-service training facilities, the two exceptions are New Zealand and Portugal in which the schools are the dominant providers of staff development while the local educational authorities do not play a role at all. In France, the Federal Republic of Germany and Japan at all levels, the local educational authorities are the most important agencies. This also holds for China, Luxembourg and Poland, which participated with only one level in the study. Other external agencies are the most important ones in Belgium-Flemish, Belgium-French, Greece, India and the Netherlands (elementary and lower secondary schools).

More insight into who the "external agencies" for the provision of staff development are can be obtained from a question to the principals of the schools. Principals were asked to indicate for each of the following (group of) agencies whether they had provided their school with support so important, that the use of computers would have clearly been different without their support. The agencies are: (1) ministry of education (federal, state, provincial); (2) local educational authorities (e.g. school board); (3) parents; (4) universities/(teacher) colleges; (5) associations (such as teacher associations, computer science associations); (6) business and industry (computer manufacturers, software developers, others); (7) support institutes (e.g. curriculum or software development institutes, local/regional resource center); (8) teachers of other schools (and 9. other). The results are summarized in Table 4.7. In comparing these results with those of Table 4.6 one should note that the respondents are different: in Table 4.6 computer coordinators and in Table 4.7 principals. For example, in the USA principals in all populations more frequently mention local educational authorities as being supportive than the computer coordinators.

The Use of Computers in Education Worldwide

Table 4.7
Percentage principals of computer using schools checking agencies giving support with teacher training

Country / Educational System

	BFL	BFR	CBC	CHI	FRA	FRG	GRE	HUN	IND	ISR	JPN	LUX	NET	NWZ	POL	POR	SLO	SWI	USA
Elementary schools																			
Ministry of education	-	23	4	-	59	-	-	-	-	46	-	-	12	16	-	11	-	-	16
Local educational author.	-	9	74	-	51	-	-	-	-	17	-	-	17	2	-	16	-	-	64
Parents	-	2	3	-	3	-	-	-	-	1	-	-	3	5	-	3	-	-	4
Universities	-	14	11	-	48	-	-	-	-	24	-	-	0	17	-	41	-	-	25
(Teacher) associations	-	28	18	-	15	-	-	-	-	6	-	-	4	15	-	6	-	-	9
Business/Industry	-	6	18	-	6	-	-	-	-	25	-	-	1	21	-	6	-	-	35
Support institutes	-	6	26	-	9	-	-	-	-	15	-	-	9	25	-	4	-	-	30
Teachers of other schools	-	24	34	-	26	-	-	-	-	5	-	-	3	34	-	12	-	-	31
Lower secondary schools																			
Ministry of education	24	31	16	-	77	81	83	-	-	-	-	89	25	24	-	21	-	82	17
Local educational author.	17	10	66	-	53	30	14	-	-	-	-	18	9	3	-	10	-	8	53
Parents	0	1	1	-	3	0	4	-	-	-	-	0	0	2	-	2	-	0	3
Universities	7	25	18	-	19	21	9	-	-	-	-	22	9	12	-	25	-	14	27
(Teacher) associations	11	14	27	-	16	11	14	-	-	-	-	19	8	20	-	4	-	21	6
Business/Industry	22	20	39	-	9	8	0	-	-	-	-	15	12	22	-	3	-	9	32
Support institutes	38	16	30	-	41	8	5	-	-	-	-	0	76	15	-	5	-	7	34
Teachers of other schools	6	15	29	-	35	7	6	-	-	-	-	22	3	30	-	5	-	21	25
Upper secondary schools																			
Ministry of education	19	24	16	17	72	83	m	13	10	58	-	-	36	23	9	23	26	47	28
Local educational. author.	17	10	66	53	54	12	m	54	12	3	-	-	10	2	32	11	31	3	64
Parents	0	0	1	6	1	0	m	0	2	1	-	-	2	0	2	3	0	0	3
Universities	11	24	18	16	16	24	m	28	5	44	-	-	13	15	22	26	15	21	43
(Teacher) associations	14	18	27	17	14	8	m	7	4	10	-	-	4	24	11	4	10	24	18
Business/Industry	22	25	39	7	34	11	m	4	6	17	-	-	22	21	6	2	16	22	39
Support institutes	39	13	30	10	46	9	m	8	59	10	-	-	51	11	5	3	52	6	37
Teachers of other schools	7	18	29	5	48	6	m	7	3	2	-	-	4	37	9	4	6	17	29

Notes. - = data not collected, m = insufficient number of cases (n<50 or missing cases >20%).

Table 4.7 shows some interesting results. Given the fact that in many educational systems higher education already has a long tradition of working with computers, the limited role of universities and (teachers) associations is remarkable; only in France and Portugal in elementary schools and in Israel in upper secondary schools universities play an important role in supporting teacher training activities. In no educational system do business and industry play a central role, although in some educational systems (for example, British Columbia and the USA) their support can be called meaningful. The role of support institutes (curriculum/software development institutes, regional centers) varies. In the Netherlands (lower secondary schools), regional centers were very important (they were part of the national stimulation policy); while also in, for example, Belgium-Flemish, British Columbia, France, India, Slovenia and the USA their role is rather important. Finally, we would like to point to the important role in all populations of teachers of other schools in British Columbia, France, New Zealand and the USA.

In summary, although educational systems differ in the way staff development is organized, we may conclude that authorities are quite supportive to staff development, not only at school level, but also at the school transcending level (local, state, provincial, national). In each country, quite a number of other agencies, such as universities and teacher training colleges, business and industry, associations and teachers of other schools are relatively important supporters as well.

Content of staff development

Teachers were asked which computer-related topics were covered during their initial or in-service teacher training. The questionnaire contained topics within five main categories: Computer and society (4 topics), Applications (14), Problem analysis and programming (5), Principles of hard- and software structure (3), and Pedagogical/instructional aspects (5). Table 4.8 presents the topics teachers reported having learned about during their training.

In lower and upper secondary schools in many educational systems, computer education teachers indicate that they learned more topics in their training than teachers of other subjects. Exceptions are British Columbia and India in upper secondary schools where the differences between the computer education teachers and the using teachers in other subjects are relatively small. At all educational levels, the using teachers of existing subjects report that they learned about more topics than the non using teachers.

Table 4.8
Percentage teachers indicating at least one topic in each category dealt with during teaching training

Country / Educational System

	BFL	BFR	CBC	CHI	FRA	FRG	GRE	HUN	IND	ISR	JPN	LUX	NET	NWZ	POL	POR	SLO	SWI	USA
Elementary schools																			
Non using teachers																			
Computer and society	-	m	m	-	m	-	-	-	-	m	13	-	m	22	-	-	-	-	36
Applications	-	m	m	-	m	-	-	-	-	m	27	-	m	36	-	-	-	-	56
Problem analysis and programming	-	m	m	-	m	-	-	-	-	m	18	-	m	16	-	-	-	-	39
Hard- and software	-	m	m	-	m	-	-	-	-	m	18	-	m	22	-	-	-	-	43
Pedagogical/instructional	-	m	m	-	m	-	-	-	-	m	12	-	m	20	-	-	-	-	35
Using teachers																			
Computer and society	-	31	38	-	44	-	-	-	-	16	28	-	29	28	-	-	-	-	52
Applications	-	49	77	-	80	-	-	-	-	37	61	-	51	66	-	-	-	-	73
Problem analysis and programming	-	64	30	-	67	-	-	-	-	40	41	-	42	21	-	-	-	-	50
Hard- and software	-	46	38	-	36	-	-	-	-	35	42	-	44	35	-	-	-	-	55
Pedagogical/instructional	-	64	49	-	64	-	-	-	-	48	49	-	m	42	-	-	-	-	40
Lower secondary schools																			
Computer teachers																			
Computer and society	58	67	m	-	-	40	96	-	-	-	43	62	77	m	-	54	-	71	66
Applications	79	88	m	-	-	58	98	-	-	-	74	88	86	m	-	70	-	83	86
Problem analysis and programming	77	94	m	-	-	68	100	-	-	-	71	88	90	m	-	60	-	76	74
Hard- and software	82	81	m	-	-	44	96	-	-	-	64	70	87	m	-	40	-	69	71
Pedagogical/instructional	49	63	m	-	-	m	42	-	-	-	41	47	m	m	-	51	-	54	63
Non using teachers*																			
Computer and society	11	m	39	-	28	m	m	-	-	-	16	46	35	22	-	41	-	50	m
Applications	21	m	63	-	60	m	m	-	-	-	38	69	50	41	-	49	-	66	m
Problem analysis and programming	27	m	34	-	64	m	m	-	-	-	32	58	54	31	-	46	-	48	m
Hard- and software	27	m	35	-	28	m	m	-	-	-	26	25	46	22	-	29	-	39	m
Pedagogical/instructional	5	m	32	-	47	m	m	-	-	-	15	19	m	15	-	33	-	24	m
Using teachers*																			
Computer and society	m	m	35	-	41	m	m	-	-	-	31	m	m	27	-	m	-	69	m
Applications	m	m	70	-	74	m	m	-	-	-	69	m	m	53	-	m	-	86	m
Problem analysis and programming	m	m	19	-	77	m	m	-	-	-	62	m	m	33	-	m	-	66	m
Hard- and software	m	m	40	-	46	m	m	-	-	-	51	m	m	37	-	m	-	59	m
Pedagogical/instructional	m	m	38	-	74	m	m	-	-	-	52	m	m	30	-	m	-	51	m

(continued on next page)

Table 4.8 (continued)
Percentage teachers indicating at least one topic in each category dealt with during teaching training

Country / Educational System

	BFL	BFR	CBC	CHI	FRA	FRG	GRE	HUN	IND	ISR	JPN	LUX	NET	NWZ	POL	POR	SLO	SWI	USA
Upper secondary schools																			
Computer teachers																			
Computer and society	53	70	43	84	56	54	75	90	69	62	61	-	m	m	75	78	m	63	57
Applications	84	89	73	79	93	69	77	85	88	81	73	-	m	m	90	76	m	84	82
Problem analysis and																			
programming	92	94	60	95	87	84	93	94	81	94	85	-	m	m	97	74	m	80	68
Hard- and software	81	87	47	78	78	66	88	92	79	89	75	-	m	m	85	75	m	72	62
Pedagogical/instructional	41	59	45	61	67	m	52	68	62	64	54	-	m	m	66	58	m	44	59
Non using teachers*																			
Computer and society	27	37	36	m	40	36	m	56	33	24	22	-	25	24	32	29	39	42	m
Applications	49	52	64	m	62	53	m	51	30	38	39	-	42	43	46	29	39	64	m
Problem analysis and																			
programming	60	65	44	m	68	58	m	54	32	53	41	-	54	32	56	25	40	51	m
Hard- and software	48	44	36	m	38	33	m	46	28	46	31	-	44	24	34	17	29	39	m
Pedagogical/instructional	26	35	31	m	44	m	m	39	17	29	16	-	m	18	33	14	21	22	m
Using teachers*																			
Computer and society	29	m	43	m	40	47	m	71	69	m	35	-	m	32	34	m	m	51	m
Applications	75	m	68	m	73	69	m	71	85	m	58	-	m	47	59	m	m	81	m
Problem analysis and																			
programming	76	m	41	m	76	74	m	82	73	m	67	-	m	50	59	m	m	67	m
Hard- and software	62	m	43	m	50	50	m	69	80	m	55	-	m	38	39	m	m	58	m
Pedagogical/instructional	45	m	46	m	69	m	m	59	56	m	42	-	m	20	31	m	m	38	m

Notes. - = data not collected, m = insufficient number of cases (n<50 or missing cases >20%),
* = (non)using teachers are teachers of existing subjects (mathematics, science or mother tongue) who do (not) use computers

The category "applications" and "problem analysis and programming" are the two most frequently mentioned topic categories dealt with during teacher training. The last topic category is especially important for computer education teachers in upper secondary schools. It is remarkable that in all teacher groups in both lower and upper secondary schools "pedagogical/instructional aspects" is one of the least mentioned topics. More detailed information about the topics covered in teacher training can be gained from Appendix C.2.

Given the differences in background data discussed before, we are not surprised to conclude from Table C.2 that elementary school teachers report fewer topics being covered in their teacher training than teachers at the other levels and that using teachers of existing subjects learned a larger number of topics than non using teachers. Another observation from these tables is the difference between non using teachers and using teachers (including computer education) in the category "pedagogical/instructional aspects": using teachers more frequently mention topics within this category than non using teachers. As "lack of software for instructional purposes" is a problem frequently mentioned by teachers and computer coordinators, it is interesting to note that the topic "locate overviews of existing software" is not frequently taught to teachers of existing subjects in lower and upper secondary schools. This result can be considered meaningful for teacher trainers because this is an activity which can be included relatively easy in teacher training activities. A final conclusion from Appendix C.2 is that there are hardly differences between lower and upper secondary schools in the content of topics in teacher training (be it initial or in-service).

Continuous staff development

Studies of successful implementation efforts have repeatedly documented the importance of ongoing interaction among innovation users during implementation (Fullan, Miles and Anderson, 1988). The study provides some information about informal interaction and communication between computer using teachers, which can be considered a form of ongoing staff development. Teachers were asked how frequently they were engaged in each of the following activities:

1. helping another teacher or being helped with problems in using software (*helping/being helped*);
2. talking generally about instructional uses of computers with another teacher (*talking instructional uses*);
3. talking about professional uses of computers (e.g. programming, recording grades, etc) with another teacher (*talking professional uses*);
4. meeting with teachers from other schools to discuss the use of computers (*meeting other schools*).

From the results presented in Table 4.9, we conclude that at all levels a majority of computer using teachers in existing subjects, as well as computer education teachers do have many informal contacts with colleagues *within* their schools; a vast majority of teachers does have these contacts during some weeks per school year. The most frequent interactions are "talking about instructional uses" and "helping/being helped". In British Columbia and the USA (upper secondary schools), more than 90% of the using teachers report having all three types of interactions within school. Although external contacts appear less frequently, teachers do have contacts with teachers of other schools. In lower and upper secondary schools in many educational systems, more than 50% of the teachers reported the existence of this kind of interaction. Teachers of existing subjects generally have less contacts with other schools than their colleagues in computer education.

Table 4.9
Percentage using teachers indicating informal interactions with other teachers

Country / Educational System

	BFL	BFR	CBC	CHI	FRA	FRG	GRE	HUN	IND	ISR	JPN	LUX	NET	NWZ	POL	POR	SLO	SWI	USA
Elementary schools																			
Using teachers																			
Helping/being helped	-	62	77	-	59	-	-	-	-	69	86	-	77	84	-	-	-	-	79
Talking instruc. uses	-	76	80	-	73	-	-	-	-	66	91	-	79	88	-	-	-	-	82
Talking prof. uses	-	56	69	-	36	-	-	-	-	30	73	-	71	52	-	-	-	-	68
Meeting other schools	-	45	41	-	36	-	-	-	-	22	54	-	38	34	-	-	-	-	28
Lower secondary schools																			
Computer teachers																			
Helping/being helped	75	75	m	-	-	72	70	-	-	-	87	86	91	96	-	89	-	93	95
Talking instruc. uses	85	85	m	-	-	92	91	-	-	-	88	89	92	92	-	95	-	94	94
Talking prof. uses	68	75	m	-	-	68	94	-	-	-	84	75	88	78	-	73	-	72	91
Meeting other schools	60	40	m	-	-	52	64	-	-	-	67	58	56	49	-	66	-	73	68
Using teachers*																			
Helping/being helped	m	m	85	-	82	80	m	-	-	-	91	m	m	77	-	m	-	90	90
Talking instruc. uses	m	m	88	-	90	91	m	-	-	-	93	m	m	77	-	m	-	93	88
Talking prof. uses	m	m	92	-	70	72	m	-	-	-	81	m	m	71	-	m	-	67	81
Meeting other schools	m	m	51	-	42	44	m	-	-	-	65	m	m	22	-	m	-	59	27
Upper secondary schools																			
Computer teachers																			
Helping/being helped	90	76	100	61	87	87	82	92	73	52	91	-	m	97	68	82	m	89	98
Talking instruc. uses	82	88	100	64	86	92	99	96	81	75	96	-	m	98	90	85	m	94	94
Talking prof. uses	78	80	97	62	73	88	95	91	69	67	95	-	m	96	69	82	m	80	94
Meeting other schools	56	54	90	64	61	52	50	88	55	48	73	-	m	63	76	48	m	62	70
Using teachers*																			
Helping/being helped	84	m	92	m	73	77	m	85	70	m	86	-	m	82	67	m	m	84	94
Talking instruc. uses	91	m	96	m	86	96	m	96	76	m	89	-	m	82	81	m	m	93	93
Talking prof. uses	69	m	96	m	73	77	m	92	66	m	90	-	m	81	57	m	m	77	90
Meeting other schools	60	m	61	m	50	28	m	63	50	m	44	-	m	29	54	m	m	59	44

Notes. - = data not collected, m = insufficient number of cases (n<50 or missing cases >20%),
* = using teachers are teachers of existing subjects (mathematics, science or mother tongue) who do use computers

Teachers' self-ratings of their knowledge and skills regarding computers

The framework presented in Chapter I shows that the knowledge and skills of teachers in handling computers is one of the factors influencing the integration of computers into existing subjects. This factor is difficult to measure (not only in cross-national but also in national surveys) as the testing of teachers in most countries is a rather controversial issue. In order to avoid controversy, we included in this study a self-rating scale consisting of a list of statements about computer related knowledge and skills, asking teachers to indicate by checking 'yes' or 'no' whether they had the knowledge or could perform the action indicated in the statement. Table 4.10 shows the statements presented to teachers.

Table 4.10
Content of self-rating scales

I know . . .(KNOWLEDGE)
1.   several advantages of computer use for instruction.
2.   the difference between a word processor and a desktop publishing program.
3.   criteria to judge the quality of a printer.
4.   the trends in hardware development in the past 20 years.
5.   what 'file extensions' are.
6.   what a 'loop' means in programming.
7.   what a 'relational database' is like.
8.   what a 'bit' is defined as.
9.   the difference between 'RAM' and 'ROM'.

I can write a program for . . .(PROGRAMMING)
1.   adding up numbers.
2.   using arrays.
3.   storing data on a disk drive.
4.   sorting data into a certain sequence.
5.   printing the complete ASCII character set.

I am capable of . . .(CAPABILITY)
1.   exchanging data between different types of computers.
2.   copying files from one disk to another.
3.   editing documents with a word processor.
4.   loading a data set from a disk drive.
5.   creating a database-file.
6.   evaluating the usefulness of software for my lessons.
7.   adapting instructional software to my needs.
8.   writing courseware for my own lessons.

Before we present the results it is necessary to say something about the presumed validity of these scales for which some evidence was collected in 1988 in England and the Federal Republic of Germany during the pilot phase of this instrument. That pilot test consisted of administering the self-rating scales in combination with a set of multiple choice items related to each of the statements in the self-rating scales. Analyses of these data showed that both measures were similar in a relative sense (namely, there were high correlations between the self-ratings and the multiple choice part), but there was also quite a high similarity in an absolute sense (almost all respondents failing on a particular multiple choice item checked 'no' on the corresponding self-rating item). Based upon these results, it was concluded that it was worthwhile to include the self-ratings in the study. Table 4.11 contains the results of the self-ratings by teachers.

Table 4.11 shows that in some educational systems the median of the percentages of the non using teachers in existing subjects on some of the scales is 0. In these cases, our data show that the mean varies between 8.5 and 31.8, which means that in these educational systems a great variation exists between teachers (that is, many teachers indicate that their knowledge and skills with computers is nil, while a smaller number knows quite a lot). The results show that using teachers in existing subjects know more than their non using colleagues. The scores for the using teachers in elementary schools are in general lower than the scores at the other levels. In this level in the scale "programming" in New Zealand and the USA the median score for both using and non using teachers is zero, which, in combination with the other low scores on this scale, is an indicator of the low priority of programming among the using teachers.

One might have expected that the computer education teachers in lower and upper secondary schools would have higher scores than the using teachers in other subjects. Although, in general, this trend can be observed, in many educational systems the scores of the using teachers do not differ appreciably from the computer education teachers (see, for example, in upper secondary schools the scale "Programming"). Some educational systems are noteworthy. In Switzerland on the scales "Programming" and "Capability" in both lower and upper secondary schools, the using teachers and the computer education teachers do have the same scores. In other educational systems, there are sizable differences between the using teachers and computer education teachers on the scale "Programming", namely in lower and upper secondary schools in New Zealand and the USA, and in upper secondary schools in Canada British Columbia and Poland. Further analysis is needed to explain this contrast in these educational systems and the much smaller differences in the other educational systems.

Table 4.11
Median percentage agreement of teachers per self-rating scale

Country / Educational System

	BFL	BFR	CBC	CHI	FRA	FRG	GRE	HUN	IND	ISR	JPN	LUX	NET	NWZ	POL	POR	SLO	SWI	USA
Elementary schools																			
Knowledge																			
Non using teachers	-	11	m	-	m	-	-	-	-	m	22	-	m	22	-	-	-	-	22
Using teachers	-	56	44	-	44	-	-	-	-	11	33	-	33	33	-	-	-	-	33
Programming																			
Non using teachers	-	0	m	-	m	-	-	-	-	m	0	-	m	0	-	-	-	-	0
Using teachers	-	50	0	-	30	-	-	-	-	0	20	-	0	0	-	-	-	-	0
Capability																			
Non using teachers	-	0	m	-	m	-	-	-	-	m	13	-	m	13	-	-	-	-	25
Using teachers	-	63	63	-	38	-	-	-	-	25	50	-	50	50	-	-	-	-	50
Lower secondary schools																			
Knowledge																			
Computer teachers	78	89	m	-	m	89	89	-	-	-	78	84	89	100	-	78	-	89	89
Non using teachers*	17	33	56	-	44	44	11	-	-	-	22	44	44	44	-	44	-	56	33
Using teachers*	m	m	56	-	67	89	m	-	-	-	67	m	m	56	-	m	-	78	56
Programming																			
Computer teachers	80	100	m	-	m	100	100	-	-	-	80	90	100	100	-	40	-	80	60
Non using teachers*	0	0	0	-	20	0	0	-	-	-	0	20	40	0	-	20	-	20	0
Using teachers*	m	m	0	-	60	80	m	-	-	-	80	m	m	20	-	m	-	80	20
Capability																			
Computer teachers	75	88	m	-	m	88	88	-	-	-	75	75	75	88	-	75	-	75	88
Non using teachers*	0	0	50	-	25	m	0	-	-	-	25	25	50	38	-	38	-	50	50
Using teachers*	m	m	75	-	63	m	m	-	-	-	75	m	m	63	-	m	-	75	63
Upper secondary schools																			
Knowledge																			
Computer teachers	100	100	100	67	89	100	89	78	67	78	89	-	m	100	89	100	m	100	89
Non using teachers*	56	44	67	m	44	67	11	33	11	33	44	-	56	44	44	33	56	67	44
Using teachers*	78	78	78	m	67	89	m	67	67	m	78	-	m	67	67	m	m	89	67
Programming																			
Computer teachers	100	100	100	100	80	100	100	100	80	100	100	-	m	100	90	100	m	100	100
Non using teachers*	60	40	20	m	40	60	0	0	0	40	40	-	40	0	20	0	0	60	20
Using teachers*	100	m	20	m	80	100	m	80	80	m	100	-	m	60	40	m	m	100	20
Capability																			
Computer teachers	75	88	100	63	75	88	88	75	75	88	75	-	m	88	88	88	m	88	88
Non using teachers*	50	25	63	m	38	63	0	0	0	25	38	-	50	50	25	13	25	50	50
Using teachers*	75	m	75	m	63	88	m	50	63	m	75	-	m	63	50	m	m	88	75

Notes. - = data not collected, m = insufficient number of cases (n<50 or missing cases >20%), for reliabilities see appendix F,
* = (non) using teachers are teachers of existing subjects (mathematics, science or mother tongue) who do (not) use computers

Another result which should be pointed to is that in many educational systems for the using teachers in existing subjects the scores on the "Programming" scale is higher than on the other two scales. Here again, further analysis is needed to explain this phenomenon.

Problems and opinions

From the perspective of implementation of computer use in education and, given the relevance of staff development for implementation, it is important to analyze what kind of problems (see Appendix D) schools and teachers experience in relation to staff development in this area. Principals, computer coordinators and teachers were asked to select from a list of about 30 problems the five they experienced as the most serious. Five of these items were related to the expertise of the school's staff or directly to staff development, namely:

1. insufficient training opportunities for teachers (*insufficient training opportunities; original item 23*);
2. teachers lack knowledge/skills about using computers for instructional purposes (*lack of knowledge/skills; original item 15*);
3. insufficient expertise/guidelines for helping teachers use computers instructionally (*insufficient help for teachers; original item 16*);
4. not enough help for supervising computer using students (*not enough student supervision; original item 11*);
5. lack of interest/willingness of teachers in using computers (*lack of interest; original item 29*).

The results are presented in Tables D.1 to D.11.

"Lack of knowledge and skills" and "insufficient training opportunities" are the two most important problems of the five mentioned. In general, teachers consider these items less frequently a problem than principals and computer coordinators (from appendix D it appears that teachers mention much more frequently time constraints). "Teachers lack interest" is apparently a rather important problem as well: for example, 51% of the principals in lower secondary schools in France report this problem, as well as at least 40% of the computer coordinators in lower and upper secondary schools in the Federal Republic of Germany.

Given this situation, it is interesting to compare these figures with the opinions of principals and teachers about the question whether in-service training courses about computers should be made compulsory. This question was stated as one of the opinion questions. For the results, presented in table 4.12, the answer categories 'agree' and 'strongly agree' are combined.

Table 4.12 shows that in many cases, principals of non using schools do not differ much in their opinion from principals of using schools. Exceptions are China and Japan, where principals of using schools are more convinced of the need to make this in-service training compulsory, while in the Netherlands and Portugal in elementary schools the reverse holds. Apparently, principals of non using schools feel that some push in this respect would be useful.

Table 4.12
Percentage of principals and teachers agreeing that in-service training should be compulsary

Country / Educational System

	BFL	BFR	CBC	CHI	FRA	FRG	GRE	HUN	IND	ISR	JPN	LUX	NET	NWZ	POL	POR	SLO	SWI	USA
Elementary schools																			
Non using principal	-	54	m	-	m	-	-	-	-	81	57	-	61	61	-	75	-	-	-
Non using teachers	-	63	m	-	m	-	-	-	-	m	36	-	m	61	-	-	-	-	44
Using principal	-	62	61	-	78	-	-	-	-	83	77	-	48	62	-	62	-	-	m
Using teachers	-	68	53	-	76	-	-	-	-	68	49	-	43	59	-	-	-	-	53
Lower secondary schools																			
Non using principal	64	m	-	-	m	m	75	-	-	-	54	-	m	m	-	66	-	37	-
Non using teachers*	44	59	53	-	63	38	86	-	-	-	33	59	43	51	-	52	-	38	51
Using principal	63	77	59	-	87	53	84	-	-	-	57	62	62	65	-	69	-	46	m
Computer teachers	66	74	m	-	-	54	95	-	-	-	60	64	61	56	-	53	-	48	70
Using teachers*	m	m	47	-	71	58	m	-	-	-	51	m	m	45	-	m	-	40	58
Upper secondary schools																			
Non using principal	m	m	-	79	m	-	74	m	86	m	m	-	61	-	74	79	m	m	-
Non using teachers*	41	55	44	m	65	42	87	41	89	70	31	-	41	50	62	53	m	37	44
Using principal	71	78	59	86	86	58	m	44	85	84	60	-	60	64	75	73	89	56	m
Computer teachers	52	67	71	95	90	51	96	56	90	83	59	-	m	56	72	58	m	53	70
Using teachers*	46	m	46	m	75	55	m	51	87	m	47	-	m	42	67	m	m	45	57

Notes. - = data not collected, m = insufficient number of cases (n<50 or missing cases >20%),
* = (non) using teachers are teachers of existing subjects (mathematics, science or mother tongue) who do (not) use computers.

Another trend is that, in general, more principals than teachers believe that in-service training should be made compulsory, although computer education teachers have a higher percentage on this variable than using teachers of existing subjects, who in general more frequently agree with the statement than their non using colleagues.

Across countries, large differences in opinions exist about making this kind of in-service training compulsory. In India almost all principals and teachers believe that in-service training on computers in education should be made compulsory, while at the other side in countries like

Japan and Switzerland, but also in Belgium-Flemish, British Columbia and the Netherlands, especially many using teachers do have an opposite or neutral opinion.

What do the results show?

When looking at the background of teachers, the results show that there are some systems (British Columbia, New Zealand and the USA) in which teachers started early in using computers, mostly receiving their first experience in computers during their student days. In general, the higher the educational level, the earlier teachers started with the use of computers at home, as well as in their teaching. Furthermore, within the group of existing subject teachers, mathematics teachers have the most experience and mother tongue teachers the least experience with computers.

Staff development activities mainly consist of introductory and application courses. In secondary schools in many systems, courses in computer science/programming and in computer use in specific subjects are available. Authorities are quite supportive of staff development. The limited role of universities and (teacher) associations in providing teacher training is remarkable.

Computer related training mainly deals with applications, problem analysis and programming. It is remarkable that pedagogical/instructional aspects are the least mentioned topics although using teachers mention these topics more often than non users.

Many teachers have informal contacts with colleagues within their schools. The knowledge and skills of computer education teachers in general are greater than that of other teachers, whereas using teachers of existing subjects know more than their non using colleagues.

In general teachers less frequently select "lack of training opportunities" and "lack of knowledge" as a problem than principals and computers coordinators. Teachers see time constraints as an important problem. The LISREL analyses in Appendix E confirm the importance of staff development for the implementation of computers in schools.

References

Akker, van den, J.J.H., Keursten, P. & Plomp, Tj. (in press). The integration of computer use in education. *International Journal of Educational Research*.

Fullan, M.G., Miles, M.B. & Anderson, S.E. (1988). *Strategies for implementing microcomputers in schools: the Ontarion Case*. Toronto, Ontarion: the Ministry of Education of Ontario, Canada.

OTA, Office of Technology Assessment (1988). *Power on! New tools for teaching and learning*. Washington DC: Government Printing Office.

Chapter V
Attitudes of principals and teachers towards computers

The introduction of computers in education is a major and complex innovation that can only succeed if - amongst others- the participants agree that it is worthwhile to be involved in. The data collected throw some light on the question how school principals and teachers think about the relevance of computers. The results show that in general principals and teachers have positive attitudes towards the educational impact of computers, but also that there is a great need for training.

About the attitude measures used in this survey

Attitudes of participants towards computers are a potential influencing factor in determining the success of implementation of computers in schools. Moreover, especially the attitudes of principals are of interest, as principals are assumed to be important change agents in a school.

In this study attitudes of principals, computer education teachers and teachers in existing subjects (mathematics, science and mother tongue) were measured by a list of respectively 15, 22 and 33 attitude items. The list of items for teachers in existing subjects is the most comprehensive list, from which subsets that were considered appropriate for the other respondents were selected. In the construction of this list three dimensions were distinguished, namely (1) Perceived Educational Impact, (2) Perceived Social Impact and (3) Training Needs. For teachers there is an additional dimension, namely (4) Self Confidence, that was excluded from the list of attitude items for principals.

The ultimate attitude scales administered in the main run were constructed after pilot testing in England, the Federal Republic of Germany, Greece and the Netherlands. The full list of attitude items is shown in Table 5.1.

As a first check on the dimensions represented in the data, the attitude data of three groups of respondents (namely, principals, computer education teachers and teachers in existing subjects) across countries were analyzed with PCA (principal component analysis) after recoding the negatively formulated statements to reflect positive statements.

Table 5.1
Content of attitude items for each category of respondents

Scale/Respondents*	Content Attitude Item
EDUCATIONAL IMPACT	
P, E	Computers are valuable tools to improve the quality of a child's education.
P, E, C	Using computers in class leads to more productivity among students.
P, E, C	Students are more attentive when computers are used in class.
P, E, C	Computers help to teach more effectively.
E, C	My way of teaching is positively affected when using a computer for teaching.
P, E, C	Computers in school enhance students' creativity.
P, E, C	The achievement of students can be increased when using computers for teaching.
E, C	A computer is not suited for teaching purposes.
E, C	Using a computer in a classroom makes a subject more interesting.
SOCIAL IMPACT	
P, E	Working with computers in class distorts the social climate.
P, E, C	Computers have become too dominant over us.
P, E	Computers harm relations between people.
P, E	Social contacts are negatively affected by the use of computers.
E	Computers reduce humans to numbers.
E, C	We will lose control over computers one day.
TRAINING NEED	
P, E, C	I try to keep myself informed about technological changes.
P, E, C	I would like to take part in a computer course to learn more about computers.
P, E, C	In-service training courses about computers should be made compulsory.
P, E, C	I would like to learn more about computers as teaching aids.
P, E, C	I don't mind learning about computers.
SELF CONFIDENCE	
E, C	Advanced technical equipment has proved difficult for me to get along with.
E	I think I can (or could learn how to) write programs on the computer.
E, C	It would take too much time to learn how to use a computer successfully.
E	I am afraid computers are too complicated for me to handle.

*: P = Principals; E = Teachers existing subjects; C = Computer education teachers

Consequently, in the abbreviated labels of the items that will be used in the section below, negative items have been reformulated to positive as well. Moreover, reliability analyses were conducted within each country for each category of respondents.

The PCA-analyses confirmed the existence of the predefined dimensions, whereas the reliability analyses (see Appendix F) showed that the reliability coefficients for each scale are quite similar across countries: the scales Educational Impact and Self Confidence have reliabilities of about .90, Social Impact between .80 and .90 and Training Need is in general the lowest with a reliability between .65 and .80, which is still quite high for a five item scale.

Attitudes of principals

In presenting the results of the attitude measures taken from principals, we will make a distinction between principals of computer using schools and principals of non using schools. Data from systems with less than 50 valid cases in a particular category were dropped (see Table B.1 in Appendix B for a list of the number of valid cases per category of respondents).

Table 5.2 contains for each category of respondents and each educational system the medians of the percentage agreement on the attitude items in each scale.

The results in Table 5.2 show as a general pattern across educational systems a high degree of agreement with the items in each scale. Some remarkable exceptions are the principals in elementary schools in France and the Netherlands (and to a lesser extent in Belgium-French) who are less positive about the educational impact of computers than their colleagues in other countries. For the Netherlands this results from the fact that many principals are uncertain about the educational impact of using computers instead of having negative opinions.

In lower secondary schools principals from Mid-European countries tend to be less positive about the educational impact of computers than their colleagues abroad, whereas in upper secondary schools this is the case in the Federal Republic of Germany, the Netherlands and Switzerland. Furthermore one may observe that especially on the scale Social Impact the Japanese and Greec principals in upper secondary schools are less positive than principals from schools in other countries.

In Table 5.2 one does not see a consistent pattern of differences for all scales and countries between principals of computer using schools and their colleagues in schools that do not use computers, although there is a trend that principals from computer using schools have more positive attitudes than principals from schools not using computers.

The Use of Computers in Education Worldwide

Table 5.2
Median percentage of agreement of principals per attitude scale

Country / Educational System

Scales/Levels	BFL	BFR	CBC	CHI	FRA	FRG	GRE	HUN	IND	ISR	JPN	LUX	NET	NWZ	POL	POR	SLO	SWI	USA
Elementary schools																			
Educational impact																			
Non using schools	-	33	m	-	m	-	-	-	-	83	67	-	17	67	-	83	-	-	m
Using schools	-	67	83	-	33	-	-	-	-	83	83	-	50	83	-	83	-	-	83
Social impact																			
Non using schools	-	50	m	-	m	-	-	-	-	50	25	-	75	75	-	75	-	-	m
Using schools	-	75	100	-	75	-	-	-	-	75	75	-	100	75	-	75	-	-	100
Training need																			
Non using schools	-	80	m	-	m	-	-	-	100	80	-	80	80	-	100	-	-	-	m
Using schools	-	80	80	-	80	-	-	-	100	80	-	80	80	-	80	-	-	-	80
Lower secondary schools																			
Educational impact																			
Non using schools	33	m	m	-	m	m	83	-	-	-	67	m	m	m	-	83	-	17	m
Using schools	50	67	83	-	67	33	m	-	-	-	67	67	50	83	-	100	-	33	83
Social impact																			
Non using schools	75	m	m	-	m	m	25	-	-	-	25	m	m	m	-	50	-	50	m
Using schools	75	75	100	-	75	m	m	-	-	-	50	75	100	75	-	75	-	50	100
Training need																			
Non using schools	80	m	m	-	m	m	100	-	-	-	80	m	m	m	-	80	-	80	m
Using schools	80	100	80	-	100	80	m	-	-	-	80	100	80	80	-	100	-	80	80
Upper secondary schools																			
Educational impact																			
Non using schools	m	m	m	83	m	m	83	m	100	m	m	-	33	m	83	67	m	m	m
Using schools	50	67	83	83	67	33	m	67	100	83	67	-	50	83	100	100	100	33	83
Social impact																			
Non using schools	m	m	m	75	m	m	0	m	50	m	m	-	100	m	75	75	m	m	m
Using schools	100	75	100	75	75	75	m	100	75	75	50	-	100	75	75	75	75	75	100
Training need																			
Non using schools	m	m	m	80	m	m	100	m	100	m	m	-	80	m	80	100	m	m	m
Using schools	100	80	80	80	100	80	m	80	100	100	80	-	80	80	80	100	100	80	100

Notes. - = data not collected, m = insufficient number of cases (n<50 or missing cases >20%). For reliabilities, see Appendix F.

Most surprising in Table 5.2 are the huge differences (which are quite consistent over populations) between systems on the scale Educational Impact: for instance in elementary schools the USA (83) versus the Netherlands (50); in lower secondary schools, the USA, British Columbia, New Zealand (83-100) versus Switzerland (33) and the Netherlands (50). On the other scales these between system differences do not show up to this extent. There is not yet a straightforward interpretation of these differences. Some first preliminary analyses showed that this might be related to some extent to the number of years schools already have experience with using computers: principals in schools that have a longer history of computer use tend to be more positive about the educational impact of using computers than principals in schools that do not have so much experience. At the other side, one should also consider (as stated above) that a low score on a scale does not necessarily reflect negative attitudes. What is further remarkable in the figures presented in Table 5.2 is the huge training need expressed by principals: there is an almost universal agreement with the items in this scale across countries and users versus non users.

Attitudes of teachers

The attitude scales for teachers contained more items than those for principals (see Table 5.1), amongst others an additional scale, namely Self Confidence (only two items for computer education teachers just like Social Impact and, hence, not included in the tables below).

Analogous to the presentation of the results of the attitude measures for principals, a distinction will be made between teachers who use computers and teachers not using computers. Furthermore we will distinguish between teachers of computer education courses (like informatics, computer literacy, etc.) and teachers in existing subjects. The latter group (containing teachers in mathematics, science and mother tongue) will be taken as a whole, as a further break down would result for some systems in a very low number of observations (see Table B.1 in Appendix B). Moreover, the category computer education teachers who are not using computers (who might be called phantom users) is not included. We found this category of teachers in secondary schools (lower and upper) in Belgium-Flemish, Greece, Japan, Portugal and Switzerland. Finally, data for systems with less than 50 cases are not included in the presentation of the results.

Table 5.3 contains for teachers the results of the attitude measures. Table 5.3 shows that teachers who are using computers are in general quite positive about the educational impact of computer use. This occurs in most educational systems, with the exception of the Netherlands and

Switzerland where the median scores are quite low.

Table 5.3
Median percentage of agreement of teachers per attitude scale

Country / Educational System

Scales/Respondents	BFL	BFR	CBC	CHI	FRA	FRG	GRE	HUN	IND	ISR	JPN	LUX	NET	NWZ	POL	POR	SLO	SWI	USA
Elementary schools																			
Educational impact																			
Non using teachers	-	33	m	-	m	-	-	-	-	m	33	-	m	56	-	-	-	-	44
Using teachers	-	67	78	-	44	-	-	-	-	78	67	-	44	78	-	-	-	-	78
Social Impact																			
Non using teachers	-	50	m	-	m	-	-	-	-	m	33	-	m	67	-	-	-	-	67
Using teachers	-	83	83	-	67	-	-	-	-	67	67	-	83	83	-	-	-	-	83
Training need																			
Non using teachers	-	80	m	-	m	-	-	-	-	m	60	-	m	80	-	-	-	-	80
Using teachers	-	80	80	-	80	-	-	-	-	80	80	-	80	80	-	-	-	-	80
Self confidence																			
Non using teachers	-	50	m	-	m	-	-	-	-	m	25	-	m	75	-	-	-	-	75
Using teachers	-	75	75	-	50	-	-	-	-	50	25	-	75	75	-	-	-	-	75
Lower secondary schools																			
Educational Impact																			
Computer teachers	63	75	m	-	m	50	100	-	-	-	63	50	38	88	-	100	-	50	100
Non using teachers[*]	22	22	56	-	22	22	67	-	-	-	33	11	22	56	-	67	-	33	56
Using teachers[*]	m	m	89	-	67	44	m	-	-	-	67	m	m	78	-	m	-	67	89
Social impact																			
Non using teachers[*]	50	50	67	-	67	50	33	-	-	-	33	33	67	83	-	83	-	50	67
Using teachers[*]	m	m	83	-	83	67	m	-	-	-	67	m	m	83	-	m	-	83	83
Training need																			
Computer teachers	80	100	m	-	m	80	100	-	-	-	80	80	80	80	-	80	-	80	100
Non using teachers[*]	80	80	80	-	80	80	100	-	-	-	60	80	80	80	-	80	-	80	80
Using teachers[*]	m	m	80	-	80	80	m	-	-	-	80	m	80	80	-	m	-	80	80
Self confidence																			
Non using teachers[*]	50	50	75	-	75	75	50	-	-	-	25	75	75	75	-	75	-	75	75
Using teachers[*]	m	m	75	-	75	100	m	-	-	-	50	m	m	75	-	m	-	75	75

(Continued on next page)

Table 5.3 (*continued*)
Median percentage of agreement of teachers per attitude scale

Country / Educational System

Scales/Respondents	BFL	BFR	CBC	CHI	FRA	FRG	GRE	HUN	IND	ISR	JPN	NET	NWZ	POL	POR	SLO	SWI	USA
Upper secondary schools																		
Educational impact																		
Computer teachers	63	63	100	88	50	50	100		88	100	75	63	m	88	88	88	m	50	100
Non using teachers*	22	22	56	m	22	22	78		44	89	56	33	22	44	67	67	78	22	56
Uusing teachers*	67	m	89	m	67	44	m		89	89	m	67	m	67	89	m	m	44	89
Social impact																		
Non using teacher*	67	50	83	m	67	67	33		83	67	67	33	83	67	67	67	33	50	67
Using teachers*	83	m	67	m	83	83	m		100	67	m	59	m	83	67	m	m	67	83
Training need																		
Computer teachers	80	80	80	80	100	80	100		80	100	100	80	m	80	80	80	m	80	100
Non using teacher*	80	80	80	m	80	80	100		60	100	80	60	80	80	80	80	80	80	80
Using teachers*	80	m	80	m	80	80	m		80	100	m	80	m	80	80	m	m	80	80
Self confidence																		
Non using teacher*	75	75	75	m	50	75	50		50	50	75	25	75	75	50	75	75	75	75
Using teachers*	100	m	100	m	75	100	m		50	75	m	50	m	100	50	m	m	75	100

Notes. - = data not collected, m = insufficient number of cases (n<50 or missing cases >20%),
*=(non)using teachers are teachers of existing subjects who do (not) use computers.

This finding is consistent with the one reported above for principals. In contrast with the findings reported for principals, the teachers that are not using computers score much lower than their computer using colleagues. Our tentative explanation is that principals have a broader -policy- view while teachers are more concrete and action oriented. This needs to be further explored in future analyses.

In most educational systems the teachers who use computers are quite positive about the social impact of computers in the sense that they generally disagree with negative statements related to this issue. Teachers not using computers are less positive with respect to this issue except for lower secondary schools in New Zealand where the scores are almost the same. The agreement with the items in the subscale "Training" is very high for using as well as non using teachers and also for computer education teachers showing that in most systems even the non computer using teachers are very interested in learning about computers, but at the other side that computer using teachers apparently consider themselves as not yet adequately trained.

In contrast with this finding it seems from Table 5.3 that teachers of existing subjects who use computers feel reasonably confident about their capacity of working with computers, while in quite a number of systems their non-using colleagues tend to feel less confident.

Although it is not surprising that computer using teachers are more self-confident, while teachers not using computers feel less self-confident, an interesting question to be addressed in future analyses will be whether any causality can be discovered between teacher perceptions of their own capacities in handling computers and their inclination to actually start to implement computers in their lessons.

For a more detailed overview of teachers' perceptions of their own competencies and skills in handling computers we refer the reader to the previous chapter.

What do the results show?

The results presented in this section show that, in general, educational practitioners have very positive attitudes about the use of computers in education. This is a reassuring finding which means that one may expect a positive influence on further implementation of computers in education. On the other hand, the results show that there is a large need for training. This finding is consistent with results reported in previous chapters, showing that lack of teacher knowledge and the insufficient facilities for teacher training are seen by many respondents as major obstacles in implementing computers in schools. The importance of this factor is further confirmed in the LISREL analyses that are reported in Appendix E, which show that staff development is one of the factors most strongly associated with implementation of computers in schools.

Chapter VI
Gender equity in relation to computers

This chapter contains a presentation of results concerning gender issues. Equal opportunities for boys and girls in computer use is important and a situation in which computer use is being perceived as a typical male activity related to mathematics and science should be avoided. Therefore, gender of principals, computer coordinators and teachers, being possible role models for students, is reviewed. In addition, special gender policies of schools, if they exist, are discussed.

The results show that, in most countries, computer use in schools is male dominated. In all systems (except the French-speaking countries) less than 50% of the schools have a special policy concerning gender issues. When having a policy, it is mostly directed to training female teachers in computer eduction.

Introduction

In many educational systems, equal educational opportunities for boys and girls is considered to be an important issue. When computers intrude all parts of society, it is a concern of many policy makers to guarantee not only equal access of boys and girls to computers, but also to provide extra stimulation to involve girls in computer related activities. The latter is considered to be important to avoid a situation in which computers are perceived by girls as being primarily for boys, or as being something only for those pupils who are good in mathematics and science, subjects for which there is research evidence that boys outperform girls.

Voogt (1987) analyzed a number of projects aimed at reducing the difference in the involvement of boys and girls in computer use and participation in computer education. From these projects many suggestions emerge, which can be ordered into several categories:
Teachers:
- more female teachers as role model;
- increase of teachers' consciousness that gender differences are indeed a problem.
Career perspective:
- pay explicit attention to career possibilities for girls.

Curriculum development:
- show many different computer applications;
- avoid a situation in which working with computers will be identified with mathematics and science activities;
- avoid gender bias in curriculum materials;
- in the case of teaching programming, select a language which is appealing to girls (there is some evidence that LOGO is more attractive for girls than, for example, BASIC).

Grouping and teaching methods:
- create "peer role models", for boys as well as girls;
- if students work in mixed groups on the computer, make sure that girls and boys spend equal time at the keyboard;
- offer teaching about the computers such, that emphasis is put on the control students have over the system.

School organization:
- make rules for accessing computers which guarantee sufficient opportunities for girls;
- if there is a computer education course, schedule it such that it is no obstacle for girls to attend.

Only limited research has been done in this area, of which the outcomes are ambiguous (Voogt, 1987). In stage 1 of the Comped study, some data with regard to gender equity were collected on the school- and teacher level, whereas in stage 2 student data will also be collected (knowledge, attitudes, and background data).

In the remainder of this chapter we will first present context data, relevant for the gender issue. Next we will describe to what extent schools have policies to stimulate equal involvement of both boys and girls in computer use.

Context characteristics of schools

Gender of students

In elementary and lower secondary schools (computer using as well as non using schools), the percentage of boys and girls in the schools is, as might be expected, almost equal varying around 50%.

Enrollment figures for boys and girls differ in only a few systems for upper secondary schools, as can be seen in Table 6.1. It is not clear whether the larger number of boys in some countries is a reflection of the opportunities of girls to participate in upper secondary education in these educational systems.

Table 6.1
Average percentage girls enrolled in using and non using upper secondary schools (as indicated by the principal)

Country / Educational System

	BFL	BFR	CBC	CHI	FRA	FRG	GRE	HUN	IND	ISR	JPN	LUX	NET	NWZ	POL	POR	SLO	SWI	USA
Upper secondary schools																			
Using schools																			
Female students	51	50	49	47	44	49	m	47	36	51	52	-	50	51	72	53	54	51	50
Non using schools																			
Female students	m	m	m	45	m	m	49	m	32	m	m	-	55	m	74	53	m	m	m

Notes. - = data not collected, m= insufficient number of cases (n<50 or missing cases >20%).

Gender of principals, computer coordinators and teachers

Table 6.2 shows the percentages of female principals, computer coordinators and teachers for computer using schools at all educational levels.

Table 6.2
Percentage female principals, coordinators and teachers in computer using schools

Country / Educational System

	BFL	BFR	CBC	CHI	FRA	FRG	GRE	HUN	IND	ISR	JPN	LUX	NET	NWZ	POL	POR	SLO	SWI	USA
Elementary schools																			
Female principals	-	30	17	-	44	-	-	-	-	61	5	-	6	17	-	58	-	-	m
Female coordinators	-	m	28	-	m	-	-	-	-	79	17	-	5	21	-	42	-	-	75
Female teachers	-	70	71	-	59	-	-	-	-	88	50	-	63	68	-	70	-	-	m
Lower secondary schools																			
Female principals	16	19	8	-	21	7	38	-	-	-	1	15	3	20	-	52	-	4	m
Female coordinators	15	m	14	-	m	5	7	-	-	-	4	4	2	22	-	23	-	3	m
Female teachers	50	54	37	-	60	42	63	-	-	-	36	37	28	48	-	65	-	33	m
Upper secondary schools																			
Female principals	16	14	8	8	18	7	m	21	27	19	4	-	5	21	32	54	31	7	m
Female coordinators	16	m	14	10	m	5	m	24	25	36	2	-	3	15	35	23	m	3	m
Female teachers	48	54	37	48	46	32	m	57	46	55	21	-	31	50	68	64	57	29	m

Notes. - = data not collected, m= insufficient number of cases (n<50 or missing cases >20%).

Some remarkable phenomena appear from these data. In most educational systems computer using elementary schools have a majority of female teachers, but most of them have only a small percentage of female computer coordinators (those persons in the school that are technically informed about computers and often responsible for the coordination of computer use).

Exceptions to this general result in elementary education are found in Israel and, to some extent, Portugal. These countries also have large percentages of female principals. In general, in these countries sufficient role models are offered: there are not only many female teachers, but females are also involved more heavily in special tasks related to the use of computers. Clearly, in countries like Japan and the Netherlands, pupils in elementary schools are not exposed to many female role models of computer coordinators. This lack of role models is even more striking if these percentages are contrasted with the percentages of female teachers.

The data for lower secondary education show that the coordination of computer activities in the schools are strongly male dominated. The lack of female role models of computer coordinators in this population as well, suggests that the professional use and application of computers is typically a male activity. Similar conclusions can be drawn for upper secondary schools.

In summary, in most countries computer use in schools is male dominated. These figures confirm the concern of many policy makers, educators and those engaged in the emancipation of girls, who believe that the daily practice of computer use in schools too strongly suggests to students that the use of computers is predominantly a matter for males and not for females. There are only a few exceptions to this trend, such as Israel and Portugal in elementary schools. Further analyses of the data may reveal whether gender patterns in computer use by students in these countries differ from countries with a strong male dominance in computer use, for example Japan and the Netherlands.

Gender policies at school level

Given the fact that educational computer use in many countries is male dominated, the question becomes relevant whether schools do have a policy focused at ensuring gender equity. Such policies may have a broad range: from explicitly organizing special activities for girls, to just providing a climate in which equal participation is presupposed and stimulated (for example by providing enough female role models).

The data presented in this section come from co-educational schools. In most countries the percentage of single sex schools is negligible (less than 4%); exceptions are in elementary education Belgium-French (7% single sex schools); in lower secondary education Belgium-Flemish (21%), Belgium-French (6%) and New Zealand (26%); and in upper secondary education Belgium-Flemish (17%), Hungary (10%), India (40%), Israel (19%), Japan (19%), New Zealand (23%), Slovenia (11%) and the USA (7%). Whether the use of computers in these countries differs between co-educational and single sex schools needs to be analyzed further.

Principals were asked whether the "school has a special policy dealing with equity of computer use by boys and girls (e.g. to encourage girls to use computers as much as boys)".

The results, presented in Table 6.3, show a great variety across countries. In all three populations, a majority of principals in computer using schools in the French speaking countries (Belgium-French, France and Luxembourg) indicate having a specific gender policy. Greece (in lower secondary schools) is the only other country with a sizeable percentage of schools having such a policy. The low percentages in countries like Portugal and Israel are as such not so surprising, as in these countries females and males are already playing almost equal roles in schools' computer activities as could be seen in table 6.2.

Table 6.3
Percentage principals of computer using co-educational schools indicating a special gender policy

Country / Educational System

	BFL	BFR	CBC	CHI	FRA	FRG	GRE	HUN	IND	ISR	JPN	LUX	NET	NWZ	POL	POR	SLO	SWI	USA
Elementary schools	-	35	3	-	65	.	.	-	.	13	14	-	32	17	-	27	.	-	m
Lower secondary schools	27	76	2	-	56	5	48	.	.	-	14	69	26	27	-	16	-	25	m
Upper secondary schools	25	73	2	14	62	5	m	30	42	17	22	-	18	26	0	9	14	12	m

Notes. - = data not collected, m = insufficient number of cases (n<50 or missing cases >20%).

From an emancipatory perspective, of more concern are the low percentages in countries like British Columbia, the Federal Republic of Germany, Japan, the Netherlands, New Zealand and Switzerland, about which we concluded earlier that the educational contexts lack sufficient female role models and computer activities are strongly male dominated. Principals of computer using co-educational schools with a special policy were asked to indicate their school's policy by selecting any of the following: (1) in-service sessions for teachers about equity are scheduled; (2) a girls computer class or instructional group was formed; (3) information is given to parents about equity in relation to computers; (4) females are selected to supervise computer activities by students; (5) out-of-class time is set aside for girls-only access to computers; (6) teachers are given specific suggestions about how to promote equity; (7) training of female teachers in computer education; (8) other ways. The results are presented in Table 6.4. Because the group of computer using co-educational schools having a gender policy is relatively small, systems are included in Table 6.4 if at least 30 cases are available.

From these results several trends emerge. In all three populations, the most practiced policy is "training of female teachers in computer education", with "females are selected to supervise computer activities by students" in the second place. Overall, two possible policies tend to be practiced least in all three populations: "out-of-class time is set aside for girls-only access to computers" and "a girls computer class or instructional group was formed". Hence, it seems that schools prefer to establish measures in which they stimulate female role models (female teachers and supervisors) rather than creating special opportunities for computer use for girls.

If we look at the results within educational systems, some interesting conclusions emerge. We already concluded that, in the French speaking countries, the majority of computer using schools do have a specific gender policy. From Table 6.4 we conclude that in these countries, in almost all populations (exception is Belgium-French in elementary schools, but included is Switzerland in lower and upper secondary schools), the main gender policy applied is training of female teachers and selection of female supervisors. Hardly any of the other policies is applied.

Notable is that in the USA next to supervision by females, two policies are particular important. These are 'in-service sessions for teachers' and 'specific suggestions to teachers'. This result indicates that in the USA, the teacher is important when dealing with gender issues. Further analysis of the American situation might give some indications about the activities the schools plan for teachers (in-service as well as other activities). Also in Japan conducting in-service sessions for teachers is an important element in the gender policy of schools.

Table 6.4
Percentage principals indicating kind of policy when their school has a gender policy

Country / Educational System

	BFL	BFR	CBC	CHI	FRA	FRG	GRE	HUN	IND	ISR	JPN	LUX	NET	NWZ	POL	POR	SLO	SWI	USA
Elementary schools																			
In-service sessions for teachers	-	11	m	-	5	-	-	-	-	m	55	-	17	37	-	m	-	-	30
Computer class for girls was formed	-	2	m	-	2	-	-	-	-	m	0	-	0	2	-	m	-	-	7
Information given to parents	-	23	m	-	4	-	-	-	-	m	19	-	21	16	-	m	-	-	12
Supervision by females	-	15	m	-	27	-	-	-	-	m	21	-	46	59	-	m	-	-	36
Time set aside for girls-only access	-	0	m	-	3	-	-	-	-	m	4	-	0	18	-	m	-	-	12
Specific suggestions to teachers	-	9	m	-	3	-	-	-	-	m	12	-	31	58	-	m	-	-	34
Comped training for female teachers	-	43	m	-	45	-	-	-	-	m	27	-	58	77	-	m	-	-	24
Lower secondary schools																			
In-service sessions for teachers	39	10	m	-	8	m	m	-	-	-	56	0	44	m	-	m	-	10	36
Computer class for girls was formed	0	1	m	-	1	m	m	-	-	-	7	0	1	m	-	m	-	3	15
Information given to parents	47	7	m	-	1	m	m	-	-	-	10	0	27	m	-	m	-	15	2
Supervision by females	39	47	m	-	31	m	m	-	-	-	5	17	46	m	-	m	-	22	34
Time set aside for girls-only access	0	0	m	-	0	m	m	-	-	-	22	0	0	m	-	m	-	1	11
Specific suggestions to teachers	46	14	m	-	8	m	m	-	-	-	51	0	39	m	-	m	-	15	32
Comped training for female teachers	39	64	m	-	67	m	m	-	-	-	37	17	86	m	-	m	-	50	16
Upper secondary schools																			
In-service sessions for teachers	37	3	m	37	9	m	m	18	45	m	55	-	60	m	-	m	m	8	56
Computer class for girls was formed	0	0	m	1	1	m	m	38	34	m	17	-	0	m	-	m	m	3	14
Information given to parents	34	4	m	9	5	m	m	60	51	m	16	-	24	m	-	m	m	0	7
Supervision by females	46	53	m	37	30	m	m	33	39	m	16	-	49	m	-	m	m	42	63
Time set aside for girls-only access	0	0	m	16	1	m	m	13	57	m	14	-	2	m	-	m	m	0	0
Specific suggestions to teachers	27	7	m	15	12	m	m	26	61	m	10	-	37	m	-	m	m	4	50
Comped training for female teachers	49	63	m	56	61	m	m	0	42	m	22	-	53	m	-	m	m	53	21

Notes. - = data not collected, m = insufficient number of cases (n<30 or missing cases >20%).

In some countries, like the Netherlands and New Zealand (in elementary schools), a broad spectrum of possible gender policies exists. Relatively frequently mentioned in New Zealand is the policy to give teachers specific suggestions to promote equity.

Relatively high in the Netherlands is the percentage on "comped training for female teachers" in lower secondary schools. This is a consequence of the national policy of having at least one female teacher being trained before schools could get their hardware configuration.

In upper secondary schools, India is the country with the broadest spectrum of gender policies in schools. In interpreting this, we should keep in mind that the Indian sample is not representative for the nation as a whole (see Appendix B). We would also point to the relative importance of "specific suggestions to teachers" and "out-of-class time that is set aside for girls-only access to computers" in the Indian sample, compared to the most important policies across countries like "training for female teachers" and "supervision by females".

Finally, we point to some other interesting patterns. The relatively low percentage in the USA for "training of female teachers" is understandable from the context characteristics, which indicates that in the USA many females already play a prominent role in computer activities at the school level. In lower secondary schools, we also point to the relatively high percentages in Belgium-Flemish on the policies "information is given to parents about equity in relation to computers" and "teachers are given specific suggestions about how to promote equity". In upper secondary schools, Hungary is a notable case: none of the schools mentions the training of female teachers (the most important gender policy on school level in most other countries) while the information given to parents is the most important.

Gender differences among principals and computer coordinators in problems experienced

The implementation of computers in schools is, at school policy level, the responsibility of the principal, and, on operational level, the responsibility of the computer coordinator. In this section, the degree to which problems experienced by principals and computer coordinators are related to gender differences is explored.

The questionnaires to principals and computer coordinators contained a list of 29 topics which could be noted as serious problems in the use of computers in the schools. From this list we selected eight topics on which some gender differences between either male and female principals and/or computer coordinators could be expected. The potential problems are (between parentheses the corresponding numbers in the original list are given; see Appendix D for the total list):

1. software too difficult or too complicated to use (6);
2. not enough help for supervising computer using students (11);
3. integration of computer use in the existing prescribed (school/class) curriculum (13);
4. teachers lack knowledge/skills about using computers for instructional purposes (15);
5. insufficient expertise/guidelines for helping teachers use computers instructionally (16);
6. not enough technical assistance for operating and maintaining computers (19);
7. insufficient training opportunities for teachers (23);
8. lack of administrative support or initiatives from a higher level of school administration (24).

Given the low number of female principals (of computer using schools) and of computer coordinators in some countries, results are only presented for those countries from which data are available from at least 30 female and 30 male principals or coordinators. The results for the principals are presented in Table 6.5 and for the computer coordinators in Table 6.6.

Generally speaking, in many cases there is not much difference between male and female principals and coordiators in the degree to which they experience certain problems. In some countries a pattern can be found. For example, in India male principals and coordinators in upper secondary schools experience more problems than their female colleagues. Across populations, male coordinators mention "integration of computer use in the existing prescribed (school/class) curriculum" more frequently as a problem than females. A problem indicated often by female coordinators is "insufficient technical operating assistance". The problems "teachers lack knowledge" and "insufficient expertise to help teachers" are mentioned relatively frequently in both sub-populations and across populations, suggesting that a lack of expertise in using computers is experienced as a major problem by both females and males.

Table 6.5
Percentage of male/female principals (users) checking a problem

Country / Educational System

	ELEMENTARY SCHOOLS						LOWER SEC. SCHOOLS				UPPER SECONDARY SCHOOLS							
	BFR	FRA	ISR	NWZ	POR	USA	BFL	FRA	POR	USA	BFL	FRA	HUN	IND	NWZ	POL	POR	USA
Software too difficult																		
Males	14	26	5	9	0	8	8	19	7	8	5	12	28	20	13	8	6	6
Females	18	27	2	9	10	5	6	27	5	5	1	11	23	10	15	12	3	1
Not enough supervising help																		
Males	38	52	22	38	39	43	15	45	58	36	10	41	36	36	23	14	49	28
Females	44	60	27	39	39	39	12	52	39	47	7	31	31	22	34	16	40	29
Integration in instruction																		
Males	60	49	36	37	75	35	39	77	63	33	38	63	81	50	67	49	60	32
Females	48	51	48	20	64	37	41	80	80	37	29	64	81	58	76	51	74	18
Teachers lack knowledge																		
Males	83	70	54	64	78	78	53	76	78	72	55	70	67	43	74	64	78	80
Females	72	81	75	61	79	73	61	78	81	75	73	72	64	39	88	63	76	75
Insuff. expertise to help teachers																		
Males	56	52	34	52	69	23	32	56	79	18	33	53	46	55	48	64	77	17
Females	60	57	57	57	78	14	27	65	75	25	42	50	45	41	62	70	73	34
Insuff. techn. operating assistance																		
Males	28	39	9	27	27	24	10	29	32	27	16	36	61	42	47	53	35	21
Females	26	52	17	31	29	18	18	29	40	32	5	39	59	27	51	53	36	14
Insufficient training opportunities																		
Males	48	48	30	53	62	49	22	33	81	42	19	33	26	67	73	37	78	45
Females	57	55	40	53	76	36	14	31	71	45	11	40	25	53	70	36	71	64
Lack of administrative support																		
Males	58	13	26	9	47	8	21	20	62	8	21	13	7	36	2	15	57	6
Females	30	20	25	12	43	7	22	15	38	3	12	14	2	18	18	11	42	3

Table 6.6
Percentage of male/female coordinators (users) checking a problem

Country / Educational System

	ELEMENTARY SCHOOLS							LOWER SEC. SCH.			UPPER SECONDARY SCHOOLS								
	CBC	FRA	ISR	JPN	NWZ	POR	USA	FRA	POR	USA	BFL	CHI	FRA	HUN	IND	ISR	POL	POR	USA
Software too difficult																			
Males	14	18	6	42	10	12	5	31	9	9	5	8	17	24	19	6	7	7	8
Females	3	16	4	42	19	0	6	29	9	1	0	12	16	12	11	6	9	6	4
Not enough supervising help																			
Males	45	51	21	27	34	40	33	40	32	28	13	17	41	38	38	22	14	37	24
Females	54	71	20	69	28	20	31	41	34	44	8	13	31	51	32	22	11	36	33
Integration in instruction																			
Males	53	43	30	47	31	60	70	77	58	63	39	46	65	82	51	62	55	59	55
Females	43	42	32	82	39	49	49	67	62	53	21	42	53	82	51	50	40	60	39
Teachers lack knowledge																			
Males	61	67	69	78	67	74	80	77	74	83	50	43	66	71	43	69	53	73	76
Females	66	74	64	75	81	72	81	73	80	81	34	58	68	79	38	59	49	76	79
Insuff. expertise to help teachers																			
Males	40	42	57	71	57	76	29	58	62	27	31	57	58	51	57	52	67	63	14
Females	40	67	46	61	52	67	33	57	67	29	35	70	55	57	47	51	70	70	28
Insuff. techn. operating assistance																			
Males	24	35	7	58	25	16	12	28	21	35	11	40	39	51	38	15	51	23	15
Females	40	39	16	91	40	30	13	30	29	26	26	53	41	60	38	23	63	28	18
Insufficient training opportunities																			
Males	30	45	51	89	62	67	57	45	63	53	23	55	43	29	64	40	34	64	48
Females	43	48	36	73	54	60	30	41	62	57	10	56	36	37	56	46	34	64	50
Lack of administrative support																			
Males	14	23	35	46	9	42	12	26	31	25	2	26	32	10	35	17	19	33	11
Females	17	25	7	58	15	17	12	27	24	11	0	34	17	7	16	20	14	31	10

Gender differences among teachers in knowledge and skills with respect to computers

Teachers working with computers, either in teaching about computers or in using computers as a tool in their instruction, need to know about computers and be able to handle computers. The gender issue is important in this respect as well: a female teacher with limited knowledge and skills will give another role model than a female teacher with broad knowledge and skills. An impression of gender differences in this respect can be obtained from three self-rating scales about computer knowledge and skills, which were included in the teacher questionnaire (see also Chapter IV). The three scales can be characterized as:

-   knowledge scale: 9 questions about knowledge of hardware and software (format of the questions: "I know ...");
-   programming scale: 5 questions about programming skills (format: "I can write a program for ...");
-   capability scale: 8 questions about the ability of using the computer as a tool for, for example, word processing and computer assisted instruction (format: "I am capable of ...").

All questions are yes/no questions; see Table 4.10 for the list of items.

The results of these measures are presented only for those countries which have at least 30 male and 30 female teachers. Table 6.7 shows the data, which are for Population 2 and 3 divided up for two different categories of teachers: computer education teachers and teachers of existing subjects using computers.

It appears that (almost) consistently at all three educational levels and on all scales, males have higher self-rating scores than females.

A closer look at the data reveals the following: in elementary schools, in which no distinction in categories of teachers is made, in most countries the median scores of the females on the programming scale is zero. The same holds for male teachers in British Columbia, the Netherlands, New Zealand and the USA; only part of the male teachers in France and Japan can write (simple) computer programs.

Table 6.7
Median percentage on knowledge and skill scales of male and female teachers (users)

Country / Educational System

	BFL	BFR	CBC	CHI	FRA	FRG	GRE	HUN	IND	ISR	JPN	LUX	NET	NWZ	POL	POR	SLO	SWI	USA
Elementary schools																			
Know-scale																			
Male	-	m	56	-	44	-	-	-	-	m	44	-	33	44	-	-	-	-	44
Female	-	m	33	-	33	-	-	-	-	m	22	-	22	33	-	-	-	-	33
Programming-scale																			
Male	-	m	0	-	40	-	-	-	-	m	20	-	0	0	-	-	-	-	0
Female	-	m	0	-	0	-	-	-	-	m	0	-	0	0	-	-	-	-	0
Capability-scale																			
Male	-	m	63	-	50	-	-	-	-	m	50	-	50	63	-	-	-	-	50
Female	-	m	50	-	25	-	-	-	-	m	38	-	25	38	-	-	-	-	50
Lower secondary schools																			
Computer teachers																			
Know-scale																			
Male	78	m	m	-	-	m	m	-	-	-	m	m	89	100	-	89	-	m	89
Female	67	m	m	-	-	m	m	-	-	-	m	m	73	78	-	56	-	m	78
Programming-scale																			
Male	80	m	m	-	-	m	m	-	-	-	m	m	100	100	-	60	-	m	80
Female	80	m	m	-	-	m	m	-	-	-	m	m	50	60	-	40	-	m	60
Capability-scale																			
Male	75	m	m	-	-	m	m	-	-	-	m	m	75	88	-	88	-	m	88
Female	63	m	m	-	-	m	m	-	-	-	m	m	63	75	-	75	-	m	75
Using teachers*																			
Know-scale																			
Male	m	m	67	-	78	m	m	-	-	-	m	m	m	78	-	m	-	m	67
Female	m	m	44	-	44	m	m	-	-	-	m	m	m	33	-	m	-	m	44
Programming-scale																			
Male	m	m	20	-	80	m	m	-	-	-	m	m	m	60	-	m	-	m	40
Female	m	m	0	-	20	m	m	-	-	-	m	m	m	0	-	m	-	m	20
Capability-scale																			
Male	m	m	75	-	75	-	m	-	-	-	m	m	m	69	-	m	-	m	75
Female	m	m	75	-	38	-	m	-	-	-	m	m	m	50	-	m	-	m	63

(continued on next page)

Table 6.7 (continued)
Median percentage on knowledge and skill scales of male and female teachers (users)

Country / Educational System

	BFL	BFR	CBC	CHI	FRA	FRG	GRE	HUN	IND	ISR	JPN	LUX	NET	NWZ	POL	POR	SLO	SWI	USA
Upper secondary schools																			
Computer teachers																			
Know-scale																			
Male	100	100	m	67	89	m	m	89	67	89	m	-	m	100	89	100	m	100	100
Female	89	89	m	56	89	m	m	78	78	78	m	-	m	89	78	100	m	78	89
Programming-scale																			
Male	100	100	m	100	100	m	m	100	80	100	m	-	m	100	100	100	m	100	100
Female	100	100	m	80	60	m	m	100	100	100	m	-	m	100	80	100	m	80	80
Capability-scale																			
Male	88	88	m	75	m	m	88	88	63	88	m	-	m	88	88	100	m	88	88
Female	75	75	m	50	75	m	m	63	75	75	m	-	m	75	75	82	m	88	88
Using teachers[*]																			
Know-scale																			
Male	m	m	m	m	78	m	m	73	67	m	m	-	m	78	m	m	m	m	67
Female	m	m	m	m	44	m	m	56	56	m	m	-	m	56	m	m	m	m	44
Programming-scale																			
Male	m	m	m	m	100	m	m	100	80	m	m	-	m	80	m	m	m	m	40
Female	m	m	m	m	20	m	m	60	80	m	m	-	m	40	m	m	m	m	20
Capability-scale																			
Male	m	m	m	m	75	m	m	63	50	m	m	-	m	75	m	m	m	m	75
Female	m	m	m	m	38	m	m	38	63	m	m	-	m	63	m	m	m	m	63

Notes. - = data not collected, m = insufficient number of cases (<30 females and/or <30 males, or missing cases >20%),
[*] using teachers are computer using teachers of existing subjects (mathematics, science and mother tongue).

The data show further that teachers in secondary education perceive their knowledge and skills as higher than their colleagues in elementary education. In lower secondary schools, male teachers score the highest on the knowledge scale and the more technical programming scale, while for female teachers in all countries the scores on the programming scale are the lowest.

What do the results show?

In most countries computer use in schools is male dominated (especially strong in Japan and the Netherlands). Exceptions are Israel, Poland and Portugal.

When asking principals whether the school has a special policy concerning gender issues, only in French-speaking countries (Belgium-French, France and Luxembourg) and in Greece (lower secondary schools) do a majority indicate having such a policy. Schools having a special gender policy mainly have training for female teachers in computer education and selection of females for supervision of computer activities as important activities. Stimulating female role models is thus the most important policy. In the French-speaking countries (with a majority of schools having a policy), the main gender policy applied is training of female teachers and selection of female supervisors, while in the USA in-service sessions for teachers and specific suggestions to teachers are more important.

When looking at gender differences in knowledge and skills of computer using teachers, at all three educational levels males have generally higher self-rating scores than females and on the knowledge, programming and capability scale.

References

Vellemann, P. F. & Hoaglin, D. C. (1981). *Applications, basics, and computing of exploratory data analysis.* Boston (MA, USA): Duxbury Press.

Voogt, J. (1987). *Vrouwen en informatica; Meisjes in het ISI-project* [Women and informatics; girls in the ISI-project] 's-Hertogenbosch (the Netherlands): PCBB.

CHAPTER VII
Summary and Discussion

This chapter reviews the major issues that have been dealt with in the previous chapters. First a summary is given and next a discussion of the major findings is presented. Although the implementation of computers in education is proceeding more slowly than some would wish, the results presented so far offer an optimistic picture, showing that computers are increasingly integrated in education. In order to optimize the use of computers in education, obstacles such as lack of software and insufficient training facilities need to be overcome.

Summary

Chapter I contained a description of the aims of the study and the conceptual framework underlying its design and instrumentation. The educational system was characterized in terms of levels of decision-making and the factors contributing to effect changes were discussed. These factors include the quality, clarity and relevance of the objectives and the characteristics of the innovation (content, materials, instructional strategies); support and leadership; staff development; experiences with innovations; and the existence of evaluation and feedback. The framework reflects the hierarchical structure of most educational systems, but acknowledges that decisions which promote or inhibit the implementation of computer-related curricula are made at all levels, which may cause discrepancies between decisions and expectations that exist at different system levels. An identification of these discrepancies may in itself be an important starting point for improvement measures in education. Furthermore Chapter I showed that altogether data were collected from about 60.000 respondents (principals, computer coordinators and teachers) in 19 educational systems. Chapter II contained a description of the availability of hardware and software and showed that once computers are available in schools they are used for instructional purposes. The rapid changes that occurred between 1985 and 1989 in the percentage of schools that had access to computers were illustrated with Figure 2.1.

The average number of computers in schools changed more gradually although, in some countries, sudden jumps could be observed as a result of (governmental) stimulation programs. Many educational practitioners still see a lack of software and hardware as the most important problems encountered in using computers.

Chapter III discussed why and how teachers use computers. Most notable is that in many countries only a small percentage of teachers in secondary schools are using computers. An exception is the USA where almost half of the teachers in secondary schools use computers in their lessons. Generally, teachers organize the use of computers in such a way that 2-3 students share the available equipment and, if necessary, the class is split up allowing one group to work with computers, while the other students perform other activities. Drill and practice is very frequently mentioned as an approach for which computers are used. Many teachers experience a lack of software and time constraints as the most serious problems in using computers in schools.

Chapter IV dealt with staff development and showed that staff development activities mainly consist of introductory and application courses. In secondary schools in many systems, courses in computer science/programming and in computer use in specific subjects are also available. Authorities are quite supportive of staff development. Computer related training mainly deals with applications, problem analysis and programming. It is noteworthy that pedagogical/instructional aspects are the least mentioned topics although using teachers mention these topics more often than non-users.

The results presented in Chapter V showed that, in general, educational practitioners have very positive attitudes about the use of computers in education. The data also showed that there is a large need for training.

Chapter VI dealt with gender equity and computers. The results showed that, in most countries, computer use in schools is male dominated (especially in Japan and the Netherlands). Exceptions are the USA, Hungary, Israel, Poland and Portugal. When principals were asked whether the school has a special policy concerning gender issues, only in French-speaking countries (Belgium-French, France and Luxembourg) and in Greece (upper secondary schools) do a majority indicate having such a policy. The gender policies of schools mainly consist of training for female teachers in Computer Education and selecting females to supervise computer activities. Stimulating female role models is thus the most important policy on school level. In the French-speaking countries (with a majority of schools having a policy), the only gender policy applied is training of female teachers and selection of female supervisors. When looking at gender differences in knowledge and skills of computer using teachers, in almost all cases at all three educational levels, males have higher self-rating scores than females on the knowledge, programming and capability scale.

Discussion

The previous chapters presented a description of the status of computer use in 1989 in 19 educational systems. The major questions addressed are whether computers are used in schools and, if so, why and how computers are used.

The results described so far show that, in many educational systems, most schools have access to computers which are used for instructional purposes. However, there are great differences within as well as between educational systems with respect to the availability of computer hardware and software as well as the conditions for use in the schools.

The results presented constitute a snapshot of the situation that existed in 1989. This situation is not stable, as some tables showed that on certain variables (like the percentage of schools using computers for instructional purposes) rapid changes took place in the five-year period preceding 1989. Other variables, such as the number of computers available in schools, showed more gradual and moderate changes, whereas on some key variables, for example, the integration of computers in existing lesson practices, changes seem to occur quite slowly.

From the description given previously one may infer that in many schools some of the most crucial conditions for a successful integration of computers (as referred to in Chapter I) are still not fulfilled: the three most important reasons for not using computers, as well as the problems experienced as most serious in using computers, are the lack of teachers' knowledge and skills and the lack of hardware and software. Given the current situation, one may wonder how the integration of computers in existing lesson practices might be improved. At this moment we only can provide a partial and tentative answer to this question based upon the LISREL analyses that were conducted by using the school-level data (that is, data from the Principal and Computer Coordinator questionnaires) from the Netherlands and the USA. A full report of these analyses is included in Appendix E. These analyses showed how some of the key variables that were presented in previous chapters are related to the degree of implementation of computers in schools. School computer education policy proved to be the most powerful predictor of innovation strategy in both the USA (0.41) and the Netherlands (0.30). Innovation experience and perceived relevance have significant effects on active innovation strategy in both countries. Although the antecedent variables failed in predicting adequately the dependent variable, implementation width, in the case of the Netherlands, nearly 50 per cent of the variance in this criterion could be accounted for in the model of the USA. The difference arises in part because the effects on implementation of innovation experience and availability are substantial in the USA but not in the Netherlands, and also because the influence of staff development policy is more substantial in the USA.

It is a promising sign that many computer using educational practitioners think very positively about the potential beneficial effects of computers, especially as practical experiences do not seem to counteract these perceptions. On the other hand, the conditions for using computers are experienced by these persons as far from optimal.

In the literature, we find many claims about the potential of computers in changing educational practices: more problem solving and greater educational productivity. The results presented in this report show that there are not yet clear signs that these latter changes are taking place at a fast rate. The data show that in many educational systems learning about computers plays an important role, whereas applications in existing subjects (if at all) frequently deal with drill and practice. Problem solving and simulation approaches, which are indicative of a more innovative approach are still rather scarce.

On basis of the data collected in the USA, Becker (1990) states:

"In the last five years, changes in how schools use computers have been modest, but the direction that these changes are taking is fairly clear. Systematic and regular student practice of basic skills in elementary school computer laboratories has become somewhat more common. But the major development in computer activity at all levels, but primarily in middle and high schools, has been a concentrated effort to use computers as productivity tools for expressing ideas and recording and analyzing information. Still, the progress in both directions has been slower than the adherents of either one would like to believe".

Real innovative changes can only take place when good quality software products are available and teachers are well acquainted with these products (by being trained in using them and integrating them into their instructional approaches). Our data show that these two conditions are hardly fulfilled: lack of software and lack of teacher knowledge and skills are among the most important problems encountered in using computers. The analyses reported in Appendix E confirm the significance of these variables in influencing the implementation of computers in schools.

References

Becker, H. J. (1990). *Computer use in the United States schools: 1989. An initial report of U.S. participation in the I.E.A. Computers in Education Survey.* Paper presented at the 1990 meetings of the American Educational Research Association.

Appendix A

Names and addresses of participants

Name and addresses of participating institutions, General Assembly members and National Project Coordinators involved in the Computers in Education Study.

Country	National Project Center	General Assembly Member	National Project Coordinator
Austria	Universität Salzburg Institut für Erziehungswissenschaft Akademiestr. 26 A-5020 Salzburg	V. Krumm	G. Haider
Belgium (Flemish)	Seminarie en Laboratorium voor Didactiek H. Dunantlaan 2 9000 Gent	J.A.P. Heene	C. Brusselmans-Dehairs
Belgium (French)	Université de Liège (Sart Tilman) B32 4000 Liege 1	G.L. De Landsheere	N. Deltour
Canada (British Columbia)	Faculty of Education University of British Columbia 2125 Main Mall V6T 1Z5 Vancouver B.C.	D. Robitaille	S. Donn
China	China's IEA national centre Central Institute of Educ.Research 46 Bei San Huan Zhong Lu Beijing	Teng Chung	H. Zhenyong

Country	National Project Center	General Assembly Member	National Project Coordinator
France	Department of Evaluation and International Comparisons 1 Avenue Léon Journault 92 311 Sevres	D. Robin	D.Robin E. Barrier
FR Germany	Institut der Pedagogik für Naturwissenschaften (IPN) Universität Kiel Olshausenstrasse 92	W. Tietze	H. Hansen
Greece	Department of Education University of Patras Patras	G. Kontogiannopoulou-Polydorides	G. Kontogiannopoulou-Polydorides
Hungary	Orszagos Pedagogia Intezet Pf. 338 Budapest 1445	Z. Báthory	P. Vári
India	Council of Educational Research and Training Sri. Aurobindo Marg. New Delhi 110016		A.K. Jalaludin
Israel	School of Education Hebrew University Jerusalem	D. Nevo	D. Davis
Italia	CEDE Villa Falconieri 00044 Frascati RM	A. Visalberghi	A.M. Caputo

Country	National Project Center	General Assembly Member	National Project Coordinator
Japan	National Institute for Educational Research of Japan 6-5-22 Shimomeguro Meguro-Ku Tokyo	H. Takizawa	T. Sawada
Luxembourg	Institut Supérieur d'Etudes et de Recherches Pedagogiques BP 002 7201 Walferdange	R. Dieschbourg	R. Dieschbourg
Netherlands	Universiteit Twente Department of Education OCTO P.O. Box 217 7500 AE Enschede	Tj. Plomp	A.C.A. ten Brummelhuis
New Zealand	Research and Statistics Division Ministry of Education P.O. Box 1666 Wellington	R.A. Garden	M. Chamberlain J. Burns
Poland	Oddzial Doskonalenia Nayczycieli IKN ul. Garbaska, 1 31-131 Krakow	B. Niemierko	H. Szaleniec
Portugal	Gabinette de Estudos e Planeamento Av. Miguel Bombarda 20 1093 Lisboa Codex	C. Climaco	M. Maia M.J. Rau

Country	National Project Center	General Assembly Member	National Project Coordinator
Slovenia	University Edvard Kardeijn Ljubljana Gerbiceva 62 P.P. 76	M. Setinc	M. Setinc
Spain	Centro de Investigation- y Documentacion Educativa Ciudad Universitaria, S/N 28040 Madrid	A. Tiana Ferrer	A. Tiana Ferrer
Switzerland	Institut für Verhaltens- wissenschaften Turnerstrasse 1 ETH-Zentrum 8092 Zürich	A. Gretler	K. Frey R. Niederer E. Ramseier
U.S.A.	Center for Social Org. of Schools Johns Hopkins University 3505 N; Charles Street Baltimore MD 21218	R.M. Wolf	H. Becker

Steering Committee

Chairman: Tj. Plomp (Netherlands)
Permanent members: R. Watanabe (Japan)
                                      R.M. Wolf (USA)
                                      W.J. Pelgrum (Netherlands)
Ad hoc members: C. O'Muircheartaigh (UK, sampling referee)
                                      H.J. Becker (USA)
                                      R.A Anderson (USA)
                                      D. Smith (UK)
                                      M. Lockheed (USA)

Appendix B

National target population and sample sizes

Belgium-Flemish

Population 2 (lower secondary education) and Population 3 (upper secondary education).
All (state, province/community and catholic) schools offering comprehensive general or comprehensive technical/arts education.

Belgium-French

Population 1 (elementary education).
All (state, province/community and catholic) schools, except special education (3,7% of all students).
Population 2 (lower secondary education).
All (state, province/community and catholic) schools offering comprehensive general or comprehensive vocational education (technical and arts). Excluded is vocational education (22,8% of all students) and special education (3,9% of all students).
Population 3 (upper secondary education).
All general secondary and vocational schools, except special education (3,9%).

Canada-British Columbia

Population 1 (elementary education), Population 2 (lower secondary education) and Population 3 (upper secondary education).
All schools.
For the Principal and Computer Coordinator questionnaires no distinction was made between Population 2 and Population 3.

China

Population 3 (upper secondary education).
All schools in the cities/provinces Beijing, Shanghai, Xingxiang city (Henon province), Inner Mongolia, Guangxi Zhuang autonomous region, Jiling, Anhui, Sichuan, Guangdong provinces.

France

> *Population 1 (elementary education).*
> All schools except private education (15% of students) and special education (less than 0,5% of students).
> *Population 2 (lower secondary education).*
> All schools except private education (students in "Collèges": 20% of all students) and special education.
> *Population 3 (upper secondary education).*
> All schools except private education (3% of students).

Federal Republic of Germany

> *Population 2 (lower secondary education) & Population 3 (upper secondary education).*
> All schools in 9 Bundesländer (58% of all students).

Greece

> *Population 2 (lower secondary education) & Population 3 (upper secondary education).*
> All schools except private and evening schools (altogether 4% of all students).

Hungary

> *Population 3 (upper secondary education).*
> All schools.

India

> *Population 3 (upper secondary education).*
> All schools in Delhi and Utter Pradesh, Maharashtra, West Bengal and Tamil Madu (which are the states with the maximum number of computer using schools (in respectively the regions NORTH, WEST, EAST AND SOUTH).

Israel

> *Population 1 (elementary education).*
> All schools except special education (7% of all students).
> *Population 3 (upper secondary education).*
> All academic schools and technological schools with courses leading
> to certification. This excludes vocational education as well as
> independent schools (about 4% of all students).

Japan

> *Population 1 (elementary education) and Population 2 (lower
> secondary education).*
> All schools except special education.
> *Population 3 (upper secondary education).*
> All general and vocational schools.

Luxembourg

> *Population 2 (lower secondary education).*
> All general and technical secondary schools.

The Netherlands

> *Population 1 (elementary education).*
> All schools except special education.
> *Population 2 (lower secondary education).*
> All schools except (5% of all students) international transition year,
> english stream, individual agricultural education, agricultural
> education and nautical education.
> *Population 3 (upper secondary education).*
> All general secondary, social nursery, economical/administrative and
> technical schools. Excluded are all other vocational schools (about
> 6.4 % of all students). Teachers were only sampled from general
> secondary schools.

New Zealand

Population 1 (elementary education).
All schools with students in <u>standard 4</u> except the Correspondence
School and special education.
Population 2 (lower secondary education).
All schools with students in <u>form 3</u>, except the Correspondence
School and special education.
Population 3 (upper secondary education).
All schools with students in <u>form 7</u>, except the Correspondence
School and special education.

Poland

Population 3 (upper secondary education).
All schools.

Portugal

Population 1 (elementary education).
All schools in the public school system of the continental territory,
except distance education.
*Population 2 (lower secondary education) & Population 3 (upper
secondary education).*
All schools in the public schools system of the continental territory.

Slovenia

Population 3 (upper secondary education).
All schools.

Switzerland

Population 1 (elementary education).
All schools in the French speaking part with students in the age of 10 years.
Population 2 (lower secondary education).
All schools except schools in canton Argau, Genève, Vaud.
Population 3 (upper secondary education).
All schools except schools in canton Genève.

USA

The sampling frame included all U.S. schools, public and private, that contained a 4th grade or higher, plus vocational and "alternative" high schools. The frame excluded separate schools for the special education population and also excluded schools that only exist to provide part-day or part-year pull-out classes for students from other schools.

Each school was allocated to one or more of three sub-frames, "primary", "lower-secondary", or "upper-secondary", depending on whether it contained a 5th grade, 7th or 8th grade, or 10th, 11th, or 12th grade.

Sixth-grade-only schools were allocated to the primary sub-frame and 9th-grade-only schools to the lower-secondary sub-frame.

Table B.1

Number of cases per educational system and category of respondents

Country / Educational System

Elementary schools	BFR	CBC	FRA	ISR	JPN	NET	NWZ	POR	USA
Principals									
non using	102	1	33	101	157	102	101	152	0
using	145	152	340	159	206	113	379	100	425
undetermined	0	1	15	0	0	14	4	3	0
Coordinators									
non using	8	0	6	0	29	1	3	10	80
using	69	136	315	156	186	125	361	90	307
undetermined	2	0	4	2	151	1	2	152	28
Teachers									
non using	153	40	21	21	664	26	61	0	163
using	75	337	188	305	370	193	329	0	271
undetermined	0	0	0	0	13	1	1	0	1

Lower secondary schools	BFL	BFR	CBC	FRA	FRG	GRE	JPN	LUX	NET	NWZ	POR	SWI	USA
Principals													
non using	61	14	0	7	26	367	99	0	19	1	114	303	0
using	221	172	138	393	382	60	264	27	237	122	150	669	415
undetermined	5	0	0	19	2	6	0	0	6	0	2	30	0
Coordinators													
non using	3	1	0	0	3	2	33	0	0	0	17	1	72
using	131	112	120	413	299	113	216	27	236	127	146	463	303
undetermined	6	3	0	0	6	39	105	0	1	1	108	6	27
Computer teachers													
non using	55	6	11	0	0	99	64	0	3	4	25	22	0
using	144	55	30	0	51	55	136	66	192	103	75	252	230
undetermined	1	0	0	0	0	1	4	1	4	0	11	2	1
Subject teachers total													
non using	226	178	327	401	244	408	811	80	404	248	116	580	356
using	24	17	100	258	219	6	178	2	48	146	38	127	235
undetermined	1	0	0	15	2	7	2	0	13	0	5	0	1
Teachers math													
non using	84	61	124	158	69	138	253	23	150	84	45	214	106
using	15	7	20	141	129	6	85	0	26	62	17	60	84
undetermined	1	0	0	3	1	2	0	0	0	0	1	0	0

(continued on next page)

Table B.1 (continued)
Number of cases per educational system and category of respondents

Country / Educational System

Lower secondary schools

	BFL	BFR	CBC	FRA	FRG	GRE	JPN	LUX	NET	NWZ	POR	SWI	USA
Teachers science													
non using	73	53	128	145	91	138	259	30	132	88	45	199	113
using	2	4	17	61	48	0	74	2	13	22	13	25	75
undetermined	0	0	0	3	0	1	2	0	9	0	3	0	1
Teachers mother tongue													
non using	69	64	75	98	84	132	299	27	122	76	26	167	137
using	7	6	63	56	42	0	19	0	9	62	8	42	76
undetermined	0	0	0	9	1	4	0	0	4	0	1	0	0

Upper secondary schools

	BFL	BFR	CBC	CHI	FRA	FRG	GRE	HUN	IND	ISR	JPN	NET	NWZ	POL	POR	SLO	SWI	USA
Principals																		
non using	6	6	0	90	4	0	426	2	408	33	49	56	0	143	65	5	16	1
using	254	192	138	329	360	198	30	306	471	151	613	160	133	429	155	74	303	424
undetermined	0	0	0	0	24	0	5	3	1	0	0	34	0	1	0	6	5	0
Coordinators																		
non using	0	0	0	3	3	1	0	0	3	0	57	0	0	2	10	0	0	31
using	224	137	118	277	359	193	29	282	469	148	549	170	138	313	155	37	282	337
undetermined	1	6	2	5	2	7	0	5	1	0	44	0	1	150	66	14	0	42
Computer teachers																		
non using	4	1	2	12	14	1	7	15	15	4	83	1	1	0	18	7	30	0
using	349	133	104	275	325	91	76	282	458	244	415	9	136	177	137	46	576	285
undetermined	2	0	0	0	4	0	4	0	0	2	3	1	0	0	6	10	8	0
Subject teachers total																		
non using	310	181	179	0	373	262	137	704	385	163	1931	97	273	297	116	129	558	311
using	57	37	77	35	168	68	2	148	295	16	209	33	138	65	44	7	140	254
undetermined	1	0	0	0	4	1	13	0	0	0	7	7	0	1	0	13	4	0
Teachers math																		
non using	130	70	74	0	139	107	45	226	140	55	510	32	80	120	50	47	167	99
using	30	23	13	19	72	41	2	61	114	5	93	24	70	23	27	1	59	77
undetermined	1	0	0	0	3	1	5	0	0	0	0	0	0	0	0	11	2	0
Teachers science																		
non using	110	68	58	0	132	102	39	204	138	59	830	35	100	154	42	30	204	97
using	17	12	28	16	78	25	0	78	167	10	103	8	53	41	14	6	60	83
undetermined	0	0	0	0	0	0	7	0	0	0	5	6	0	1	0	1	1	0
Teachers mother tongue																		
non using	70	43	47	0	102	53	53	274	107	49	591	30	93	23	24	52	187	115
using	10	2	36	0	18	2	0	9	14	1	13	1	15	1	3	0	21	94
undetermined	0	0	0	0	1	0	1	0	0	0	2	1	0	0	0	1	1	0

Appendix C

Selected tables

Table C.1
Percentage of teachers of existing subjects indicating the use of particular software at home or in school (by themselves and/or students)

Country / Educational System

Elementary schools	TEACHERS OR STUDENTS								TEACHER AND STUDENTS							
	BFR	CBC	FRA	ISR	JPN	NET	NWZ	USA	BFR	CBC	FRA	ISR	JPN	NET	NWZ	USA
Drill practice	65	73	74	93	54	78	71	94	65	71	71	88	52	75	68	87
Tutorial programs	22	48	18	30	33	49	53	74	20	40	15	25	30	48	48	58
Word processing	53	90	43	30	45	48	90	75	26	84	38	24	2	16	85	53
Painting drawing	19	39	28	23	35	19	30	33	15	29	26	18	20	14	25	15
Music composition	3	12	16	4	13	6	11	11	1	8	16	2	7	3	9	2
Simulation	7	30	7	7	25	16	46	48	7	26	7	6	15	13	43	33
Recreational games	26	42	52	26	29	57	66	78	22	35	51	23	19	53	60	50
Educational games	39	60	63	52	23	73	89	90	38	56	62	45	18	71	86	78
BASIC	46	14	60	12	37	26	30	46	28	7	50	6	6	13	22	26
LOGO	77	26	78	29	16	15	40	36	70	22	73	21	6	10	35	21
Other progr. lang.	8	5	3	4	11	5	10	9	0	2	1	2	0	1	5	3
Spreadsheet	12	23	11	4	29	12	17	20	3	3	3	2	1	1	6	4
Math. graphing	14	11	11	9	13	10	24	18	9	7	9	7	3	4	19	12
Statistics	4	9	3	1	25	3	11	7	0	1	1	0	1	1	7	0
Database	18	26	6	11	19	16	28	25	5	9	2	7	1	2	20	11
Lab interfaces:	3	3	2	2	2	6	2	2	3	1	2	1	0	0	1	0
Control devices	0	6	2	0	8	2	6	10	0	2	1	0	0	2	5	6
Control int.video	0	3	1	0	3	0	2	3	0	1	0	0	1	0	2	0
CAD/CAM	4	3	1	1	2	0	4	2	0	2	0	1	1	0	4	0
Computer communic.	1	14	4	0	8	3	5	7	0	6	1	0	1	0	4	2
Tools/utilities	15	15	13	2	17	14	41	19	3	2	7	0	0	4	14	8

Lower secondary schools	TEACHERS OR STUDENTS							TEACHER AND STUDENTS						
	CBC	FRA	FRG	JPN	NWZ	SWI	USA	CBC	FRA	FRG	JPN	NWZ	SWI	USA
Drill practice	38	95	61	79	48	62	82	31	94	50	42	43	54	61
Tutorial programs	35	35	18	48	43	46	69	28	33	9	26	34	35	45
Word processing	92	38	66	84	69	84	78	72	11	44	4	43	65	38
Painting drawing	41	11	24	51	28	57	36	26	3	13	10	12	32	3
Music composition	10	1	3	8	9	15	13	3	0	1	2	4	3	0
Simulation	25	11	18	51	41	20	51	15	9	8	17	32	9	31
Recreational games	28	17	22	30	47	35	69	14	14	19	5	34	23	29
Educational games	32	33	21	24	61	25	78	21	29	19	10	51	20	56
BASIC	19	50	66	59	30	44	50	5	31	56	3	13	22	15
LOGO	4	26	8	8	26	24	25	1	17	5	0	21	8	4
Other progr. lang.	7	13	3	14	15	18	17	0	1	0	1	3	2	0
Spreadsheet	43	21	35	60	34	55	41	8	3	17	1	5	23	5
Math. graphing	15	20	39	26	29	30	26	10	8	24	6	16	13	10
Statistics	9	10	10	44	27	18	19	1	5	2	2	8	6	4
Database	25	19	31	44	28	43	33	4	4	14	0	9	13	3
Lab interfaces:	5	3	4	3	3	1	11	3	1	0	1	1	0	4
Control devices	3	0	8	6	3	5	7	1	0	5	0	2	2	1
Control int.video	2	1	0	3	1	0	5	1	0	0	0	1	0	0
CAD/CAM	3	1	3	7	6	10	8	0	0	1	1	2	2	3
Computer communic.	16	2	2	11	5	9	11	1	0	1	0	2	1	2
Tools/utilities	19	21	16	24	42	33	20	3	3	4	1	6	2	2

(continued on next page)

Table C.1 (continued)
Percentage of teachers of existing subjects indicating the use of particular software at home or in school (by themselves and/or students)

Country / Educational System

Upper secondary schools	TEACHERS OR STUDENTS									
	BFL	CBC	FRA	HUN	IND	JPN	NWZ	POL	SWI	USA
Drill practice	32	45	67	45	64	25	33	54	31	68
Tutorial programs	19	52	23	36	48	15	44	58	26	66
Word processing	46	87	42	34	73	46	62	6	79	84
Painting drawing	11	35	12	36	40	27	14	26	41	39
Music composition	4	5	3	19	35	9	1	14	7	10
Simulation	25	31	28	46	49	22	52	34	43	50
Recreational games	7	26	12	34	50	15	23	17	14	60
Educational games	5	23	21	39	57	11	26	25	10	62
BASIC	23	21	43	49	65	37	40	17	50	51
LOGO	4	13	12	14	49	3	14	14	13	18
Other progr. lang.	16	16	28	22	36	22	17	15	42	24
Spreadsheet	19	39	34	22	51	47	41	34	58	51
Math. graphing	54	29	40	41	60	24	55	26	46	47
Statistics	23	16	23	26	37	36	47	9	29	27
Database	12	38	25	18	49	42	34	14	47	41
Lab interfaces:	12	10	15	14	9	4	11	5	9	22
Control devices	9	9	2	15	4	11	3	2	13	15
Control int.video	2	6	4	6	4	0	1	2	1	10
CAD/CAM	2	6	4	7	8	5	5	2	14	8
Computer communic.	0	19	6	7	1	10	5	8	11	19
Tools/utilities	14	29	27	14	8	31	50	9	35	31

Upper secondary schools	TEACHERS AND STUDENTS									
	BFL	CBC	FRA	HUN	IND	JPN	NWZ	POL	SWI	USA
Drill practice	26	44	65	40	56	21	28	46	25	37
Tutorial programs	14	43	22	30	39	12	39	38	19	34
Word processing	21	60	6	16	55	4	29	3	46	44
Painting drawing	2	12	1	25	33	4	3	22	16	5
Music composition	0	3	0	15	27	3	1	12	2	0
Simulation	16	22	21	32	41	11	47	26	30	29
Recreational games	0	13	7	32	42	6	8	17	6	14
Educational games	2	17	17	34	46	7	18	22	6	25
BASIC	14	6	25	41	53	8	26	12	38	15
LOGO	2	8	5	9	39	0	2	9	8	3
Other progr. lang.	9	5	8	11	25	2	8	11	24	3
Spreadsheet	9	8	14	14	35	3	23	22	19	9
Math. graphing	39	23	29	26	47	3	47	22	26	33
Statistics	14	3	17	11	27	1	41	5	14	10
Database	0	10	6	7	34	0	13	8	10	6
Lab interfaces:	11	6	8	8	7	0	10	2	6	15
Control devices	9	4	1	9	4	1	2	0	8	4
Control int.video	2	4	1	6	3	0	0	0	1	0
CAD/CAM	2	4	3	7	7	0	0	0	4	3
Computer communic.	0	8	1	7	1	0	1	3	1	5
Tools/utilities	2	5	6	7	4	0	13	5	6	10

Note. countries with less than 50 cases not included.

Table C.2
Percentage elementary school teachers not using computers indicating for each topic whether they learned about it during teacher and/or in-service training.

Country / Educational System

	JPN	NWZ	USA
Computers and society			
History/evolution	8	7	24
Relevance	8	16	17
Impact of applications	6	7	17
Ethical issues	6	15	18
Applications			
Editing/word processing	19	25	40
Drawing/painting etc.	14	13	20
Spreadsheets	13	7	15
Database management	7	9	14
Statistical applic.	11	2	8
Artificial intelligence	1	2	4
Authoring languages	9	4	6
Models and simulations	4	4	10
Laboratory instrumentation	5	2	6
Scanning/image processing	7	2	6
CAD/CAM/process control	1	2	4
Telecommunication etc.	1	2	5
Educ./recreational games	8	29	43
Music generation	2	4	9
Problem analysis and programming			
General concepts	11	9	24
General procedures	8	5	14
Structure of programs	10	11	28
Programming languages	15	7	24
Problem analysis	8	5	11
Principles of hard- and software structure			
Basic computer concepts	18	22	41
Hardware	8	4	19
Software	8	4	22
Pedagogical/instructional aspects			
Drill/practice programs	7	7	26
Overviews of exist. softw.	7	9	12
Evaluation of software	3	11	21
Integr. software in lesson	4	11	16
Organ. of computer use	4	16	11

(continued on next page)

Table C.2 (continued)
Percentage computer using teachers of elementary schools indicating for each topic whether they learned about it during teacher and/or in-service training.

Country / Educational System

	BFR	CBC	FRA	ISR	JPN	NET	NWZ	USA
Computers and society								
History/evolution	16	17	25	5	14	14	13	43
Relevance	15	18	19	6	15	19	19	31
Impact of applications	23	22	33	9	15	19	15	26
Ethical issues	15	28	20	4	20	13	17	26
Applications								
Editing/word processing	46	73	59	19	44	39	58	61
Drawing/painting etc.	16	32	34	16	39	19	19	23
Spreadsheets	11	22	20	4	24	14	13	23
Database management	26	26	12	14	18	13	17	23
Statistical applic.	8	7	4	1	19	2	3	6
Artificial intelligence	3	3	6	1	3	0	2	1
Authoring languages	25	6	9	9	41	11	4	3
Models and simulations	7	9	6	1	19	2	13	17
Laboratory instrumentation	0	2	2	0	12	0	2	6
Scanning/image processing	3	2	3	1	16	0	1	4
CAD/CAM/process control	5	2	10	0	2	1	2	2
Telecommunications etc.	3	17	14	0	10	5	6	9
Educ./recreational games	25	43	51	27	27	43	39	53
Music generation	7	11	14	1	12	5	6	7
Problem analysis and programming								
General concepts	49	16	42	21	28	25	14	34
General procedures	16	13	9	3	19	4	6	17
Structure of programs	46	20	26	28	26	28	12	35
Programming languages	56	15	53	27	32	23	9	30
Problem analysis	39	10	32	10	22	8	5	12
Principles of hard- and software structure								
Basic computer concepts	36	35	28	29	40	42	32	53
Hardware	34	17	13	11	18	13	9	26
Software	23	16	14	15	21	15	18	29
Pedagogical/instructional aspects								
Drill/practice programs	57	39	42	42	39	-	24	53
Overviews of exist. softw.	28	16	22	22	31	-	13	24
Evaluation of software	34	27	31	19	21	-	24	35
Integr. software in lesson	30	24	31	29	31	-	22	33
Organ. of computer use	31	23	19	23	32	-	30	27

(continued on next page)

Table C.2 (continued)
Percentage computer education teachers of lower secondary schools indicating for each topic whether they learned about it during teacher and/or in-service training.

Country / Educational System

	BFL	BFR	FRG	GRE	JPN	LUX	NET	POR	SWI	USA
Computers and society										
History/evolution	44	44	28	96	35	52	56	31	63	53
Relevance	39	29	28	89	24	36	63	39	50	45
Impact of applications	50	52	28	93	24	53	60	40	57	46
Ethical issues	32	29	34	65	28	44	54	21	46	54
Applications										
Editing/word processing	70	81	46	91	44	82	80	61	79	79
Drawing/painting etc.	12	31	14	27	37	39	30	54	61	42
Spreadsheets	42	58	38	75	40	50	74	57	69	62
Database management	46	58	42	95	21	65	64	45	66	63
Statistical applic.	12	8	14	15	29	24	30	30	19	15
Artificial intelligence	4	10	6	9	7	29	27	4	15	13
Authoring languages	6	35	8	33	46	20	50	9	14	18
Models and simulations	9	8	14	2	32	39	58	15	21	33
Laboratory instrumentation	1	2	10	2	22	8	10	3	6	18
Scanning/image processing	2	12	2	5	20	12	6	7	18	15
CAD/CAM/process control	11	12	10	5	5	23	26	9	24	13
Telecommunications etc.	8	15	10	9	12	30	39	7	24	33
Educ./recreational games	15	37	12	35	22	35	32	42	42	54
Music generation	5	8	6	15	7	11	6	3	21	26
Problem analysis and programming										
General concepts	61	83	60	91	62	76	79	39	57	65
General procedures	31	35	42	82	49	55	37	9	29	55
Structure of programs	68	75	50	84	51	71	70	36	55	59
Programming languages	65	92	60	100	65	82	81	42	68	66
Problem analysis	58	83	36	95	46	73	67	24	59	50
Principles of hard- and software structure										
Basic computer concepts	76	63	44	95	63	65	84	31	61	67
Hardware	68	73	32	89	38	55	66	24	54	53
Software	56	31	26	82	37	35	65	13	52	54
Pedagogical/instructional aspects										
Drill/practice programs	35	52	-	35	38	35	-	34	37	52
Overviews of exist. softw.	5	35	-	16	33	11	-	7	24	35
Evaluation of software	10	25	-	18	24	9	-	21	20	51
Integr. software in lesson	10	21	-	7	30	14	-	39	27	43
Organ. of computer use	23	23	-	18	29	17	-	22	24	35

(continued on next page)

Table C.2 (continued)
Percentage lower secondary school teachers not using computers indicating for each topic whether they learned about it during teacher and/or in-service training.

Country / Educational System

	BFL	CBC	FRA	JPN	LUX	NET	NWZ	POR	SWI
Computers and society									
History/evolution	8	19	9	10	29	25	12	25	39
Relevance	5	23	11	8	18	26	16	34	33
Impact of applications	5	21	18	7	26	22	12	23	35
Ethical issues	3	21	10	7	23	17	8	10	21
Applications									
Editing/word processing	15	50	35	24	46	39	27	36	62
Drawing/painting etc.	2	20	14	16	23	9	6	14	39
Spreadsheets	10	29	20	17	15	28	15	23	45
Database management	9	19	20	11	24	20	11	13	37
Statistical applic.	3	8	5	14	21	17	12	16	13
Artificial intelligence	0	3	5	2	11	8	3	3	7
Authoring languages	1	3	10	11	5	14	3	5	4
Models and simulations	1	7	5	8	10	21	7	7	6
Laboratory instrumentation	0	4	2	12	4	4	4	3	2
Scanning/image processing	0	2	4	7	6	4	1	0	6
CAD/CAM/process control	0	4	5	2	9	7	3	2	10
Telecommunications etc.	0	10	8	2	14	11	4	5	7
Educ./recreational games	7	26	36	9	29	18	11	19	28
Music generation	0	8	7	2	9	2	2	3	13
Problem analysis and programming									
General concepts	21	24	49	23	31	42	23	36	28
General procedures	9	16	15	16	15	19	12	8	10
Structure of programs	22	23	36	20	33	42	22	28	30
Programming languages	23	25	53	27	43	51	24	39	38
Problem analysis	19	16	40	18	21	35	17	25	29
Principles of hard- and software structure									
Basic computer concepts	27	32	25	25	24	45	21	26	33
Hardware	12	15	10	9	8	25	11	16	22
Software	10	12	11	11	4	24	12	10	23
Pedagogical/instructional aspects									
Drill/practice programs	3	21	40	8	14	-	6	21	16
Overviews of exist. softw.	0	12	12	9	6	-	3	6	8
Evaluation of software	1	18	14	3	0	-	6	8	7
Integr. software in lesson	0	11	16	7	5	-	6	10	7
Organ. of computer use	1	8	8	7	5	-	7	18	7

(continued on next page)

Table C.2 (continued)
Percentage computer using teachers of lower secondary schools indicating for each topic whether they learned about it during teacher and/or in-service training.

Country / Educational System

	CBC	FRA	JPN	NWZ	SWI
Computers and society					
History/evolution	17	24	25	17	60
Relevance	21	21	13	19	54
Impact of applications	24	31	16	15	53
Ethical issues	25	19	18	16	49
Applications					
Editing/word processing	61	53	44	41	80
Drawing/painting etc.	29	26	38	9	62
Spreadsheets	34	38	35	15	69
Database management	22	33	20	10	60
Statistical applic.	8	15	21	10	20
Artificial intelligence	2	12	6	3	10
Authoring languages	5	23	46	4	6
Models and simulations	5	8	30	6	19
Laboratory instrumentation	1	4	21	1	2
Scanning/image processing	1	3	18	2	7
CAD/CAM/process control	1	8	2	4	21
Telecommunications etc.	11	14	7	9	18
Educ./recreational games	25	42	17	17	30
Music generation	4	9	6	0	18
Problem analysis and programming					
General concepts	14	64	47	27	46
General procedures	8	25	40	22	20
Structure of programs	13	42	43	24	48
Programming languages	13	68	56	25	55
Problem analysis	7	57	40	24	45
Principles of hard- and software structure					
Basic computer concepts	38	38	49	36	48
Hardware	9	26	25	23	39
Software	15	25	24	22	38
Pedagogical/instructional aspects					
Drill/practice programs	24	66	39	17	30
Overviews of exist. softw.	11	26	30	9	20
Evaluation of software	19	35	19	14	19
Integr. software in lesson	25	39	33	19	26
Organ. of computer use	20	22	30	18	27

(continued on next page)

Table C.2 (continued)
Percentage computer education teachers of upper secondary schools indicating for each topic whether they learned about it during teacher and/or in-service training.

Country / Educational System

	BFL	BFR	CBC	CHI	FRA	FRG	GRE	HUN	IND	ISR	JPN	POL	POR	SWI	USA
Computers and society															
History/evolution	47	60	31	83	38	44	69	86	51	44	55	68	74	58	45
Relevance	36	43	24	62	29	34	56	76	30	37	46	40	67	44	38
Impact of applications	37	58	34	62	42	31	55	63	48	42	47	20	61	47	42
Ethical issues	32	43	31	11	35	39	28	45	16	26	39	28	42	37	45
Applications															
Editing/word processing	65	72	53	34	74	43	49	55	68	32	53	57	72	71	72
Drawing/painting etc.	15	23	26	52	15	12	12	58	43	18	40	53	35	33	32
Spreadsheets	61	57	39	40	75	31	41	57	49	40	45	79	58	65	60
Database management	64	66	38	56	73	50	56	59	52	44	34	38	58	60	53
Statistical applic.	17	30	12	44	14	16	21	47	29	26	33	7	38	16	18
Artificial intelligence	9	22	16	5	21	17	12	18	8	24	10	3	22	28	12
Authoring languages	20	48	16	14	19	3	31	29	14	21	44	11	18	10	19
Models and simulations	21	26	21	5	11	36	12	54	18	36	30	26	28	26	25
Laboratory instrumentation	11	7	3	3	4	18	5	37	11	20	29	10	12	6	10
Scanning/image processing	6	8	17	3	5	3	3	23	5	12	28	12	15	12	8
CAD/CAM/process control	20	14	12	4	13	10	8	20	7	9	21	5	24	21	10
Telecommunications etc.	17	17	45	3	29	12	19	24	4	15	21	6	22	27	28
Educ./recreational games	8	32	15	27	18	3	19	64	58	22	25	44	39	18	37
Music generation	3	7	4	1	3	2	5	33	35	4	6	37	8	8	15
Problem analysis and programming															
General concepts	83	93	46	89	78	77	89	90	63	88	80	93	68	63	59
General procedures	61	67	40	85	43	73	72	86	43	77	76	79	44	34	49
Structure of programs	80	89	42	84	57	76	81	91	59	87	76	82	65	63	56
Programming languages	91	92	56	94	73	81	93	93	65	93	84	92	68	76	61
Problem analysis	84	91	43	81	75	66	91	91	46	89	70	94	64	69	45
Principles of hard- and software structure															
Basic computer concepts	78	80	45	66	66	52	83	76	73	86	73	66	75	63	56
Hardware	73	82	31	66	56	53	76	88	52	85	55	53	67	60	48
Software	68	57	29	57	48	41	77	85	53	81	54	77	62	58	47
Pedagogical/instructional aspects															
Drill/practice programs	27	48	20	45	42	-	39	55	42	54	26	54	45	24	43
Overviews of exist. softw.	8	40	17	20	31	-	16	38	17	34	42	32	16	17	30
Evaluation of software	12	31	34	27	24	-	24	32	26	33	28	48	28	19	47
Integr. software in lesson	20	29	24	21	40	-	20	35	23	37	30	23	38	23	35
Organ. of computer use	22	24	19	39	25	-	32	41	35	38	34	32	37	21	28

(continued on next page)

Table C.2 (continued)
Percentage upper secondary school teachers not using computers indicating for each topic whether they learned about it during teacher and/or in-service training.

Country / Educational System

	BFL	BFR	CBC	FRA	FRG	HUN	IND	ISR	JPN	NET	NWZ	POL	POR	SLO	SWI
Computers and society															
History/evolution	21	21	23	18	21	44	23	13	16	16	15	25	19	28	33
Relevance	13	15	23	14	24	45	19	11	10	19	15	18	25	29	28
Impact of applications	12	27	24	27	19	31	21	11	10	13	11	4	16	20	29
Ethical issues	12	19	22	18	25	19	5	3	11	10	7	7	8	9	19
Applications															
Editing/word processing	35	31	52	34	35	16	19	16	26	31	30	27	24	18	55
Drawing/painting etc.	6	10	16	12	14	24	11	9	16	6	4	25	8	12	28
Spreadsheets	22	12	36	24	16	24	6	13	22	23	11	40	11	16	37
Database management	20	20	25	24	25	18	10	11	14	11	10	10	5	18	30
Statistical applic.	9	20	14	11	11	18	8	11	17	11	10	2	7	10	15
Artificial intelligence	2	5	6	8	5	5	1	4	2	1	1	1	1	2	7
Authoring languages	8	17	4	12	4	10	4	9	11	10	4	2	0	12	5
Models and simulations	10	15	12	9	16	18	7	10	10	15	6	11	1	5	13
Laboratory instrumentation	6	7	5	10	16	13	4	5	15	3	2	3	2	1	6
Scanning/image processing	2	5	5	4	3	4	1	1	9	2	1	4	0	1	6
CAD/CAM/process control	5	3	5	7	4	3	2	0	2	2	2	1	2	3	9
Telecommunications etc.	2	6	13	9	7	3	2	1	2	5	5	1	2	0	11
Educ./recreational games	9	17	22	27	11	39	18	16	7	10	15	19	15	12	12
Music generation	4	6	5	4	3	19	13	1	2	2	2	12	2	0	4
Problem analysis and programming															
General concepts	48	53	31	54	54	44	22	41	34	43	23	47	13	30	35
General procedures	24	19	26	19	35	35	16	20	26	17	11	34	2	17	17
Structure of programs	48	53	33	39	41	44	22	45	30	32	23	38	13	24	33
Programming languages	54	59	35	57	43	48	24	47	38	51	25	48	24	34	45
Problem analysis	44	53	24	51	25	43	11	39	26	29	18	38	12	27	34
Principles of hard- and software structure															
Basic computer concepts	48	36	34	33	31	36	26	43	30	43	22	27	13	26	32
Hardware	27	32	18	19	26	37	14	33	13	20	12	16	8	21	25
Software	22	15	18	18	22	37	12	26	15	22	15	26	3	18	23
Pedagogical/instructional aspects															
Drill/practice programs	18	30	21	35	-	33	8	23	8	-	10	29	9	18	13
Overviews of exist. softw.	2	7	10	11	-	14	4	16	9	-	3	15	3	5	8
Evaluation of software	8	5	20	12	-	9	6	13	6	-	7	15	4	2	6
Integr. software in lesson	12	10	15	17	-	16	6	14	6	-	9	14	8	8	9
Organ. of computer use	12	8	9	5	-	17	7	11	5	-	8	18	10	6	6

(continued on next page)

Table C.2 (continued)
Percentage computer using teachers of upper secondary schools indicating for each topic whether they learned about it during teacher and/or in-service training.

Country / Educational System

	BFL	CBC	FRA	FRG	HUN	IND	JPN	NWZ	POL	SWI
Computers and society										
History/evolution	24	24	25	39	65	49	29	27	26	41
Relevance	16	29	19	18	66	31	21	23	11	34
Impact of applications	20	28	28	19	46	47	18	19	7	44
Ethical issues	13	28	22	32	33	14	24	12	11	29
Applications										
Editing/word processing	56	59	53	32	32	64	35	32	30	67
Drawing/painting etc.	11	28	19	15	41	42	28	8	34	31
Spreadsheets	45	37	40	23	47	43	32	20	54	52
Database management	44	24	33	35	35	43	24	13	20	49
Statistical applic.	22	16	19	19	36	27	28	10	8	22
Artificial intelligence	11	7	14	10	11	8	8	2	0	17
Authoring languages	16	8	16	5	17	9	31	8	5	14
Models and simulations	29	14	24	32	39	22	31	14	13	28
Laboratory instrumentation	13	8	22	23	26	14	27	6	2	13
Scanning/image processing	15	1	9	2	9	5	20	2	7	14
CAD/CAM/process control	13	5	6	8	8	4	5	3	0	17
Telecommunications etc.	9	17	14	13	7	3	9	5	2	15
Educ./recreational games	16	25	30	11	53	55	21	12	11	16
Music generation	7	7	6	5	29	38	4	0	13	10
Problem analysis and programming										
General concepts	65	28	64	65	76	55	61	37	48	50
General procedures	35	20	31	53	63	33	48	28	30	25
Structure of programs	65	25	45	60	72	54	53	36	41	48
Programming languages	71	26	70	69	78	59	62	46	48	56
Problem analysis	65	20	58	40	77	32	46	35	44	50
Principles of hard- and software structure										
Basic computer concepts	58	38	43	47	56	72	51	36	25	51
Hardware	45	21	29	37	64	41	34	22	15	42
Software	42	25	31	32	65	44	36	22	33	40
Pedagogical/instructional aspects										
Drill/practice programs	42	32	55	-	52	41	30	12	25	22
Overviews of exist. softw.	7	16	19	-	32	17	28	5	13	11
Evaluation of software	16	26	25	-	24	24	18	10	13	14
Integr. software in lesson	16	26	34	-	31	20	27	10	11	18
Organ. of computer use	22	17	16	-	35	29	24	10	20	18

Appendix D

Problems in using computers and reasons for not using computers

This appendix contains an overview of problems encountered by different groups of respondents in using computers as well as reasons for not using computers for those who were not using computers at the time of data collection. In the tables, the reasons/problems have been abbreviated. However, the full text as used in the questionnaires is given below.

MASTER LIST OF PROBLEMS IN USING COMPUTERS / REASONS FOR NOT USING COMPUTERS

Hardware

1. insufficient number of computers available
2. insufficient number of peripherals (e.g. printer)
3. difficulty in keeping computers and peripherals in working order
4. limitations of computers (e.g. out-of-date, incompatible with current software, to slow, insufficient memory, etc.)

Software

5. not enough software for instructional purposes available
6. software too difficult or too complicated to use
7. software not adaptable enough for this school's courses
8. manuals and support materials poorly designed, incomplete or inappropriate
9. lack of information about software or its quality
10. most of the software is not available in the language of instruction

Instruction

11. not enough help for supervising computer using students/teachers
12. difficult to integrate computers in classroom instruction practices of teachers
13. integration of computer use in the existing prescribed (school/class) curriculum is difficult
14. computers are inappropriate for the age level of students
15. teachers lack knowledge / skills about using computers for instructionalpurposes
16. insufficient expertise / guidelines for helping teachers use computers instructionnally

Organization / administration

17. no room in the school time-table for students to learn about or to use computers
18. not enough space to locate computers appropriately
19. not enough technical assistance for operating and maintaining computers
20. computers are only available outside the school or the school building
21. problems in scheduling enough computer time for different classes / this class
22. computers not accessible enough for teachers' / my own use
23. insufficient training opportunities for teachers
24. lack of administrative support or initiatives from a higher level of school administration
25. inadequate financial support
26. computers do not fit in the educational policy of the school

Miscellaneous

27. not enough time to develop lessons in which computers are used
28. teachers had bad experiences with other innovations
29. lack of interest / willingness of teachers in using computers

Table D.1
Percentage principals in elementary schools including a problem in their top five selection of serious problems in using computers

Country / Educational System

Problems	BFR	CBC	FRA	ISR	JPN	NET	NWZ	POR	USA
1. Insuff. computers	52	64	54	36	46	73	69	63	58
2. Insuff. periph.	10	26	8	13	18	16	24	17	37
3. Diffic. mainten.	8	16	30	14	0	0	13	3	6
4. Limitations comp.	4	10	25	18	12	21	5	8	12
5. Insuff.softw.	32	35	19	34	62	46	34	38	25
6. Softw. difficult	2	1	5	1	3	3	4	1	5
7. Softw. not adapt.	13	3	11	3	29	26	5	4	5
8. Poor qual. manuals	3	1	6	4	4	4	13	1	1
9. Lack info. softw.	5	7	13	9	14	6	15	3	9
10. Softw.not instruct.lang.	2	8	1	3	0	3	3	6	0
11. Not enough superv.	14	24	30	7	2	25	17	7	23
12. Integr. instruc.	25	20	16	19	5	14	11	12	18
13. Integr. curric.	4	7	4	11	6	13	3	24	15
14. Inappr.stud. age	2	1	0	1	0	0	0	0	1
15. Teachers lack knowledge	46	43	49	46	49	23	46	38	56
16. Insuff. exp. help	26	16	18	26	13	19	32	31	6
17. Insuff. time learn about	7	11	12	31	8	9	2	40	18
18. Computer location	27	31	14	3	14	22	13	25	20
19. Techn. operat.ass.	11	12	20	8	15	6	11	2	10
20. Comp. outside school	8	1	5	5	3	0	0	0	1
21. Schedule time	15	22	17	32	7	14	24	17	18
22. Access teachers	5	13	1	5	17	4	7	1	8
23. Insuf. training	30	21	30	20	47	11	36	50	25
24. No admin. support	19	3	6	12	10	4	3	19	3
25. Inadeq.fin. supp.	38	35	15	30	40	37	30	42	21
26. No fit school pol.	5	0	2	0	1	2	0	5	1
27. Time develop less.	18	20	28	22	42	42	22	14	36
28. Teach. innov. exper.	-	-	-	-	-	-	-	-	-
29. Teach. lack inter.	29	7	12	14	8	13	7	7	18

Notes. -: data not collected, countries with less than 50 cases not included.

Table D.2
Percentage principals in lower secondary schools including a problem in their top five selection of serious problems in using computers

Country / Educational System

	BFL	BFR	CBC	FRA	FRG	GRE	JPN	LUX	NET	NWZ	POR	SWI	USA
1. Insuff. computers	43	50	53	37	18	32	50	17	37	62	70	40	63
2. Insuff. periph.	21	14	27	7	5	13	15	13	14	24	27	14	37
3. Diffic. mainten.	2	5	10	18	3	16	4	13	7	14	3	4	8
4. Limitations comp.	13	5	7	18	12	8	9	26	2	8	11	14	15
5. Insuff.softw.	32	34	39	13	21	37	36	9	53	20	41	33	25
6. Softw. difficult	3	1	0	4	5	6	7	0	10	1	2	5	1
7. Softw. not adapt.	15	6	11	17	3	12	12	4	34	2	4	11	8
8. Poor qual. manuals	2	3	8	3	5	23	4	0	4	2	2	7	2
9. Lack info. softw.	6	12	11	14	5	17	10	18	6	7	7	8	4
10. Softw.not instruct.lang.	8	4	2	0	0	27	0	26	2	1	3	4	0
11. Not enough superv.	5	4	13	20	0	2	11	4	7	6	10	2	24
12. Integr. instruc.	18	33	30	39	29	27	11	13	25	19	23	25	19
13. Integr. curric.	14	11	16	9	10	17	12	26	14	6	8	19	11
14. Inappr.stud. age	0	0	0	0	0	0	0	0	0	0	0	0	1
15. Teachers lack knowledge	39	50	47	43	42	23	61	26	29	49	41	40	50
16. Insuff. exp. help	14	30	26	19	13	19	9	18	12	14	33	14	7
17. Insuff. time learn about	17	9	4	18	18	29	15	9	27	3	27	15	19
18. Computer location	18	9	9	15	9	10	17	13	9	18	17	18	23
19. Techn. operat.ass.	4	8	14	12	8	6	14	39	12	17	7	3	8
20. Comp. outside school	1	2	0	0	1	6	3	0	0	0	1	6	0
21. Schedule time	14	19	25	28	17	4	7	44	18	41	12	12	23
22. Access teachers	9	2	14	2	7	8	27	13	3	4	3	4	16
23. Insuf. training	14	23	25	17	8	42	38	13	10	43	41	8	23
24. No admin. support	9	11	5	8	10	6	14	0	1	0	15	3	2
25. Inadeq.fin. supp.	43	42	31	8	17	33	42	4	31	51	41	10	27
26. No fit school pol.	1	0	0	0	1	4	0	0	0	0	8	2	1
27. Time develop less.	24	28	21	25	19	25	33	18	41	36	12	36	32
28. Teach. innov. exper.	-	-	-	-	-	-	-	-	-	-	-	-	-
29. Teach. lack inter.	27	30	11	51	33	4	17	0	14	11	16	11	17

Notes. -: data not collected, countries with less than 50 cases not included.

Table D.3
Percentage principals in upper secondary schools including a problem in their top five selection of serious problems in using computers

Country / Educational System

	BFL	BFR	CBC	CHI	FRA	FRG	HUN	IND	ISR	JPN	NET	NWZ	POL	POR	SLO	SWI	USA
1. Insuff. computers	44	51	53	54	49	19	36	59	44	47	44	53	31	72	54	28	65
2. Insuff. periph.	32	16	27	35	18	8	31	16	17	18	16	22	23	26	7	11	33
3. Diffic. mainten.	4	4	10	29	16	3	16	23	16	9	11	12	35	4	11	12	8
4. Limitations comp.	20	4	7	25	12	14	23	6	24	19	8	17	15	10	16	22	14
5. Insuff.softw.	30	31	39	57	22	25	48	32	38	47	39	32	55	35	41	19	18
6. Softw. difficult	2	1	0	0	1	4	4	3	0	7	4	0	1	1	6	8	0
7. Softw. not adapt.	13	9	11	4	9	3	6	11	10	19	21	13	10	5	10	8	14
8. Poor qual. manuals	7	5	8	8	4	11	13	5	2	5	6	1	23	1	4	13	3
9. Lack info. softw.	8	16	11	8	10	8	8	10	13	11	6	10	11	8	6	8	12
10. Softw.not instruct.lang.	4	0	2	10	1	0	6	13	5	3	2	0	5	3	2	3	0
11. Not enough superv.	2	6	13	2	16	2	7	7	6	11	12	5	1	8	6	6	14
12. Integr. instruc.	20	34	30	18	29	34	34	21	29	9	24	27	15	20	24	20	16
13. Integr. curric.	13	12	16	6	10	8	15	12	23	8	12	7	8	7	16	24	11
14. Inappr.stud. age	0	1	0	1	0	1	0	2	3	0	0	4	1	0	0	0	0
15. Teachers lack knowledge	41	45	47	26	38	41	37	23	43	35	29	34	37	45	39	37	58
16. Insuff. exp. help	13	24	26	13	14	10	9	25	24	13	8	11	28	31	19	11	8
17. Insuff. time learn about	10	13	4	1	10	20	16	31	18	18	18	3	12	25	12	12	12
18. Computer location	19	15	9	3	36	5	25	9	8	18	15	13	10	21	7	19	15
19. Techn. operat.ass.	4	4	14	15	21	8	28	14	7	10	26	17	25	6	7	7	8
20. Comp. outside school	0	1	0	0	0	0	1	1	3	0	0	0	2	1	3	1	0
21. Schedule time	21	15	25	8	17	13	15	19	22	20	17	34	5	13	17	23	19
22. Access teachers	6	3	14	2	7	5	2	7	7	13	7	9	14	3	10	3	11
23. Insuf. training	12	18	25	28	19	3	6	39	13	34	7	41	13	40	5	11	34
24. No admin. support	9	10	5	9	7	2	0	13	7	4	3	0	5	13	10	3	3
25. Inadeq.fin. supp.	54	42	31	67	24	14	31	27	39	39	37	52	37	46	62	4	32
26. No fit school pol.	2	0	0	0	0	3	1	8	1	1	0	0	1	9	3	1	0
27. Time develop less.	15	19	21	5	20	18	33	37	18	42	48	31	23	13	10	30	33
28. Teach. innov. exper.	-	-	-	-	-	-	-	-	-	-	-	-	-	-	-	-	-
29. Teach. lack inter.	26	27	11	5	27	32	17	7	24	8	13	16	29	14	26	14	18

Notes. -: data not collected, countries with less than 50 cases not included.

Table D.4
Percentage computer coordinators in elementary schools including a problem in their top five selection of serious problems in using computers

Country / Educational System

	BFR	CBC	FRA	ISR	JPN	NET	NWZ	POR	USA
1. Insuff. computers	58	61	46	34	29	70	65	67	54
2. Insuff. periph.	13	22	8	21	15	24	29	21	32
3. Diffic. mainten.	6	15	26	14	4	1	11	2	10
4. Limitations comp.	12	16	23	29	18	15	5	20	11
5. Insuff.softw.	54	32	21	47	75	57	45	48	32
6. Softw. difficult	4	3	5	4	3	7	3	0	0
7. Softw. not adapt.	13	3	11	5	23	19	4	7	4
8. Poor qual. manuals	4	2	6	2	8	6	8	3	2
9. Lack info. softw.	13	7	11	7	13	7	18	8	5
10. Softw.not instruct.lang.	3	2	0	3	1	0	2	10	0
11. Not enough superv.	10	27	22	5	4	17	11	7	18
12. Integr. instruc.	31	19	11	18	6	24	14	26	26
13. Integr. curric.	-	-	-	-	-	-	-	-	-
14. Inappr.stud. age	0	0	1	0	0	0	0	0	0
15. Teachers lack knowledge	43	40	37	45	47	26	48	40	57
16. Insuff. exp. help	21	20	13	27	11	19	31	34	6
17. Insuff. time learn about	5	9	11	34	10	12	3	33	0
18. Computer location	24	28	14	5	9	19	14	24	17
19. Techn. operat.ass.	13	9	25	6	12	10	10	4	22
20. Comp. outside school	2	1	4	4	0	0	0	0	0
21. Schedule time	14	26	22	26	3	5	24	14	15
22. Access teachers	1	5	2	13	7	5	7	0	3
23. Insuf. training	22	18	32	20	42	9	40	32	19
24. No admin. support	21	5	8	3	11	4	3	14	8
25. Inadeq.fin. supp.	26	29	24	27	40	36	38	28	26
26. No fit school pol.	2	0	2	1	2	5	0	14	1
27. Time develop less.	32	31	30	22	47	29	21	15	30
28. Teach. innov. exper.	-	-	-	-	-	-	-	-	-
29. Teach. lack inter.	25	13	14	18	12	18	13	11	22

Notes. -: data not collected, countries with less than 50 cases not included.

Table D.5
Percentage computer coordinators in lower secondary schools including a problem in their top five selection of serious problems in using computers

	Country / Educational System												
	BFL	BFR	CBC	FRA	FRG	GRE	JPN	LUX	NETNWZ	POR	SWI	USA
1. Insuff. computers	33	34	32	36	22	14	61	26	33	38	68	31	52
2. Insuff. periph.	20	16	8	4	16	13	11	11	11	18	28	7	24
3. Diffic. mainten.	4	7	4	22	8	23	5	48	9	20	5	9	11
4. Limitations comp.	16	9	10	18	24	8	9	30	10	13	21	22	16
5. Insuff.softw.	50	38	27	18	30	55	65	59	53	34	55	37	36
6. Softw. difficult	0	2	1	5	5	3	4	0	17	4	4	9	1
7. Softw. not adapt.	25	10	3	13	4	10	14	4	20	5	8	12	9
8. Poor qual. manuals	8	11	7	4	9	41	7	0	6	5	8	13	5
9. Lack info. softw.	9	15	7	13	14	18	20	4	8	17	12	8	6
10. Softw.not instruct.lang.	9	2	0	1	1	29	0	22	3	1	10	6	0
11. Not enough superv.	5	7	12	16	4	5	11	7	10	9	9	5	14
12. Integr. instruc.	14	14	34	24	29	18	10	11	28	19	19	22	22
13. Integr. curric.	-	-	-	-	-	-	-	-	-	-	-	-	-
14. Inappr.stud. age	3	0	0	0	0	0	1	0	0	0	0	1	0
15. Teachers lack knowledge	30	29	52	32	2	13	40	19	38	49	32	35	54
16. Insuff. exp. help	18	20	17	14	6	22	4	0	6	21	26	14	9
17. Insuff. time learn about	17	17	14	29	29	24	22	26	26	11	22	12	0
18. Computer location	8	5	13	16	6	5	19	22	6	12	14	15	15
19. Techn. operat.ass.	6	5	13	12	14	20	7	18	14	13	5	3	22
20. Comp. outside school	3	0	0	0	1	3	0	0	0	0	1	2	0
21. Schedule time	10	17	22	25	6	3	4	7	13	27	7	17	17
22. Access teachers	7	7	16	2	3	5	11	0	5	7	1	3	7
23. Insuf. training	16	33	36	28	2	60	30	11	5	39	34	9	29
24. No admin. support	10	14	12	11	7	20	9	22	6	3	7	7	6
25. Inadeq.fin. supp.	20	26	30	14	21	27	37	11	17	26	43	10	26
26. No fit school pol.	2	3	1	1	0	11	0	0	2	1	9	2	0
27. Time develop less.	30	36	38	31	19	22	44	26	48	33	12	42	32
28. Teach. innov. exper.	-	-	-	-	-	-	-	-	-	-	-	-	-
29. Teach. lack inter.	26	37	23	37	40	5	10	7	28	39	19	14	20

Notes. -: data not collected, countries with less than 50 cases not included.

Table D.6
Percentage computer coordinators in upper secondary schools including a problem in their top five selection of serious problems in using computers

Country / Educational System

	BFL	BFR	CBC	CHI	FRA	FRG	HUN	IND	ISR	JPN	NET	NWZ	POL	POR	SWI	USA
1. Insuff. computers	41	39	33	42	38	14	24	59	41	46	28	43	21	69	26	50
2. Insuff. periph.	27	17	8	33	16	12	32	16	19	16	9	18	21	31	6	19
3. Diffic. mainten.	5	8	4	35	14	7	13	22	18	6	9	18	35	5	12	9
4. Limitations comp.	19	10	11	38	11	24	29	10	28	17	13	14	14	17	31	18
5. Insuff.softw.	36	35	26	58	23	26	47	34	40	44	44	25	56	55	28	30
6. Softw. difficult	1	2	1	1	3	4	3	5	2	4	3	0	1	2	9	1
7. Softw. not adapt.	15	5	4	4	7	3	6	11	8	17	17	9	6	7	4	8
8. Poor qual. manuals	13	6	7	6	6	8	19	7	9	6	6	5	30	7	14	5
9. Lack info. softw.	4	12	7	8	9	18	15	10	9	12	15	14	14	11	8	6
10. Softw.not instruct.lang.	7	6	0	14	0	1	5	10	7	1	3	0	3	8	4	0
11. Not enough superv.	3	3	11	1	12	3	9	9	6	17	15	6	3	8	11	10
12. Integr. instruc.	19	19	34	14	22	30	33	20	23	5	17	26	17	20	17	21
13. Integr. curric.	-	-	-	-	-	-	-	-	-	-	-	-	-	-	-	-
14. Inappr.stud. age	5	1	0	0	0	1	1	4	2	2	0	0	0	0	1	0
15. Teachers lack knowledge	30	26	53	16	29	2	38	19	48	29	23	45	25	33	32	51
16. Insuff. exp. help	13	26	18	19	18	3	14	24	24	12	14	13	27	26	17	6
17. Insuff. time learn about	16	13	14	3	23	28	14	34	30	11	22	10	9	23	15	0
18. Computer location	10	10	13	2	22	6	21	8	5	17	13	14	12	20	13	16
19. Techn. operat.ass.	6	4	13	17	25	15	16	14	6	10	17	21	29	3	7	19
20. Comp. outside school	2	1	0	0	0	1	0	2	2	1	0	0	1	1	1	0
21. Schedule time	10	18	22	18	17	6	12	20	21	14	12	31	6	8	20	15
22. Access teachers	11	7	16	1	9	3	5	7	10	12	9	12	11	1	4	7
23. Insuf. training	11	27	36	26	26	1	8	37	15	34	14	50	16	31	8	31
24. No admin. support	5	9	12	10	11	8	2	13	6	5	3	1	6	7	8	5
25. Inadeq.fin. supp.	30	29	30	59	21	26	30	24	27	43	26	40	34	39	5	31
26. No fit school pol.	4	3	1	1	0	0	2	8	2	2	0	0	0	9	2	0
27. Time develop less.	31	38	38	7	30	17	34	36	15	51	54	39	31	12	33	37
28. Teach. innov. exper.	-	-	-	-	-	-	-	-	-	-	-	-	-	-	-	-
29. Teach. lack inter.	27	18	22	4	24	45	25	7	32	12	21	25	34	18	17	30

Notes. -: data not collected, countries with less than 50 cases not included.

Table D.7
Percentage teachers in elementary schools including a problem in their top five selection of serious problems in using computers

Country / Educational System

	BFR	CBC	FRA	ISR	NETNWZ		USA
1. Insuff. computers	44	50	55	38	69	69	56
2. Insuff. periph.	21	19	9	7	15	26	22
3. Diffic. mainten.	9	11	22	12	4	13	6
4. Limitations comp.	9	8	23	18	12	6	11
5. Insuff.softw.	47	28	16	31	51	37	30
6. Softw. difficult	3	2	6	4	2	4	1
7. Softw. not adapt.	9	2	10	6	29	5	7
8. Poor qual. manuals	3	4	5	4	5	9	2
9. Lack info. softw.	20	7	17	12	7	15	4
10. Softw.not instruct.lang.	8	1	0	2	2	2	0
11. Not enough superv.	14	28	25	15	22	20	20
12. Integr. instruc.	18	27	14	11	18	16	26
13. Integr. curric.	11	13	3	4	11	11	14
14. Inappr.stud. age	2	1	1	0	1	0	0
15. Teachers lack knowledge	26	30	34	30	21	39	32
16. Insuff. exp. help	26	20	10	24	14	21	11
17. Insuff. time learn about	14	19	8	34	21	6	20
18. Computer location	9	26	12	1	16	20	16
19. Techn. operat.ass.	11	11	22	9	4	9	5
20. Comp. outside school	5	0	7	6	1	1	1
21. Schedule time	24	37	25	21	9	30	31
22. Access teachers	3	8	5	13	2	12	7
23. Insuf. training	23	17	31	15	11	31	19
24. No admin. support	6	4	3	3	4	3	4
25. Inadeq.fin. supp.	21	18	17	10	20	18	16
26. No fit school pol.	-	-	-	-	-	-	-
27. Time develop less.	41	35	46	24	31	29	40
28. Teach. innov. exper.	-	-	-	-	-	-	-
29. Teach. lack inter.	15	4	9	5	11	5	5

Notes. -: data not collected, countries with less than 50 cases not included.

Table D.8
*Percentage computer teachers in lower secondary schools including a
problem in their top five selection of serious problems in using
computers*

Country / Educational System

	BFL	GRE	JPN	LUX	NET	NWZ	POR	SWI	USA
1. Insuff. computers	35	23	41	17	36	57	63	32	34
2. Insuff. periph.	20	26	14	28	19	37	26	19	40
3. Diffic. mainten.	8	17	5	38	15	39	8	13	22
4. Limitations comp.	16	6	12	53	12	14	3	24	29
5. Insuff.softw.	32	58	58	8	37	27	54	32	35
6. Softw. difficult	3	4	5	9	17	4	2	8	2
7. Softw. not adapt.	24	9	16	13	24	6	5	8	8
8. Poor qual. manuals	10	49	7	15	7	26	14	12	11
9. Lack info. softw.	10	19	8	8	8	8	18	7	9
10. Softw.not instruct.lang.	19	34	1	8	6	1	15	10	0
11. Not enough superv.	8	8	8	8	13	12	8	4	23
12. Integr. instruc.	5	6	5	0	13	1	12	8	0
13. Integr. curric.	7	4	16	4	0	1	18	12	5
14. Inappr.stud. age	1	0	0	2	2	0	0	2	0
15. Teachers lack knowledge	21	4	37	6	20	9	12	9	5
16. Insuff. exp. help	18	32	15	8	11	8	18	10	8
17. Insuff. time learn about	8	19	15	4	20	3	49	16	18
18. Computer location	5	2	8	17	5	19	26	10	16
19. Techn. operat.ass.	6	15	7	38	9	16	6	4	11
20. Comp. outside school	1	4	3	0	0	0	0	6	0
21. Schedule time	17	4	15	2	14	8	20	15	12
22. Access teachers	7	0	8	6	3	9	2	6	4
23. Insuf. training	15	40	39	4	7	22	11	7	14
24. No admin. support	8	9	8	4	8	2	0	6	7
25. Inadeq.fin. supp.	13	17	41	13	16	29	29	10	29
26. No fit school pol.	-	-	-	-	-	-	-	-	-
27. Time develop less.	32	40	56	17	49	30	35	37	16
28. Teach. innov. exper.	-	-	-	-	-	-	-	-	-
29. Teach. lack inter.	12	6	14	13	19	14	5	10	16

Notes. -: data not collected, countries with less than 50 cases not included.

Table D.9

Percentage computer teachers in upper secondary schools including a problem in their top five selection of serious problems in using computers

Country / Educational System

	BFL	BFR	CBC	CHI	FRA	FRG	GRE	HUN	IND	ISR	JPN	NWZ	POL	POR	SWI	USA
1. Insuff. computers	32	25	31	51	41	10	13	34	58	33	39	37	17	74	24	31
2. Insuff. periph.	30	40	27	36	30	21	17	42	18	22	23	38	21	38	13	31
3. Diffic. mainten.	6	19	21	37	21	11	19	13	26	22	9	37	43	13	19	20
4. Limitations comp.	20	21	20	30	19	40	25	25	7	23	21	35	12	20	31	34
5. Insuff.softw.	30	41	29	49	18	40	48	40	34	28	42	29	52	41	20	32
6. Softw. difficult	3	6	1	0	4	0	14	2	6	2	7	4	1	1	9	3
7. Softw. not adapt.	9	10	4	3	8	3	6	4	11	10	17	3	14	9	6	11
8. Poor qual. manuals	21	20	38	11	17	21	42	30	7	25	13	22	43	20	26	22
9. Lack info. softw.	11	17	14	10	19	10	20	15	13	11	14	19	11	15	10	11
10. Softw.not instruct.lang.	12	9	0	16	1	0	43	11	15	8	3	1	9	19	6	0
11. Not enough superv.	7	3	14	2	10	2	1	12	10	12	16	6	1	6	13	17
12. Integr. instruc.	9	6	5	6	4	14	6	9	16	5	5	0	5	1	4	0
13. Integr. curric.	8	6	6	7	4	3	3	12	9	7	6	0	4	7	6	1
14. Inappr.stud. age	1	0	0	1	2	0	0	2	3	5	2	0	1	2	1	0
15. Teachers lack knowledge	16	6	4	4	11	2	3	7	12	3	23	10	10	5	5	7
16. Insuff. exp. help	24	13	6	25	16	0	38	7	23	9	14	7	37	16	5	6
17. Insuff. time learn about	10	8	4	3	7	8	7	8	36	29	14	1	2	37	21	17
18. Computer location	10	6	9	1	23	5	3	20	6	5	9	12	10	20	10	16
19. Techn. operat.ass.	8	10	18	23	21	25	22	17	14	6	12	27	36	6	7	9
20. Comp. outside school	0	1	0	0	0	0	0	0	2	6	1	0	1	0	1	1
21. Schedule time	13	7	8	15	12	8	1	16	22	23	11	7	3	18	13	8
22. Access teachers	11	5	5	3	14	0	3	4	6	7	7	6	13	4	4	6
23. Insuf. training	12	13	27	26	33	2	39	9	34	9	32	28	17	14	9	19
24. No admin. support	4	3	5	13	3	6	4	1	15	4	10	7	5	6	6	6
25. Inadeq.fin. supp.	17	17	35	54	14	24	26	28	26	18	36	34	35	32	8	26
26. No fit school pol.	-	-	-	-	-	-	-	-	-	-	-	-	-	-	-	-
27. Time develop less.	23	29	40	10	31	5	22	42	37	19	52	50	22	13	30	19
28. Teach. innov. exper.	-	-	-	-	-	-	-	-	-	-	-	-	-	-	-	-
29. Teach. lack inter.	13	10	9	9	5	10	1	15	6	18	14	14	25	5	7	12

Notes. -: data not collected, countries with less than 50 cases not included.

Table D.10

Percentage existing subjects teachers in lower secondary schools including a problem in their top five selection of serious problems in using computers

Country / Educational System

	CBC	FRA	FRG	JPN	NWZ	SWI	USA
1. Insuff. computers	44	41	22	24	47	39	56
2. Insuff. periph.	17	6	12	12	20	9	27
3. Diffic. mainten.	11	25	7	3	12	2	8
4. Limitations comp.	7	21	10	14	12	17	10
5. Insuff.softw.	46	44	26	62	39	56	37
6. Softw. difficult	1	5	3	8	7	4	2
7. Softw. not adapt.	7	28	1	23	10	13	10
8. Poor qual. manuals	3	6	11	5	4	6	5
9. Lack info. softw.	10	16	14	16	16	8	10
10. Softw.not instruct.lang.	1	0	2	2	2	4	0
11. Not enough superv.	16	16	5	7	12	6	20
12. Integr. instruc.	17	16	23	8	14	15	21
13. Integr. curric.	7	16	11	16	7	13	11
14. Inappr.stud. age	1	0	0	0	1	0	0
15. Teachers lack knowledge	20	18	3	37	23	10	15
16. Insuff. exp. help	16	10	9	15	12	4	5
17. Insuff. time learn about	15	22	30	22	10	24	15
18. Computer location	8	9	3	6	9	7	23
19. Techn. operat.ass.	7	11	7	9	12	1	6
20. Comp. outside school	0	0	2	1	0	3	3
21. Schedule time	41	40	14	12	52	21	32
22. Access teachers	15	8	5	5	13	5	12
23. Insuf. training	13	11	5	37	26	3	12
24. No admin. support	1	3	6	5	3	5	6
25. Inadeq.fin. supp.	10	4	9	18	20	10	18
26. No fit school pol.	-	-	-	-	-	-	-
27. Time develop less.	34	35	12	57	42	44	29
28. Teach. innov. exper.	-	-	-	-	-	-	-
29. Teach. lack inter.	2	7	22	15	8	6	5

Notes. -: data not collected, countries with less than 50 cases not included.

Table D.11
Percentage existing subjects teachers in upper secondary schools including a problem in their top five selection of serious problems in using computers

Country / Educational System

	BFL	CBC	FRA	HUN	IND	JPN	NWZ	POL	SWI	USA
1. Insuff. computers	38	35	37	28	56	31	38	33	27	54
2. Insuff. periph.	19	13	10	22	14	12	14	20	11	27
3. Diffic. mainten.	6	13	10	6	28	4	14	13	4	5
4. Limitations comp.	11	13	21	16	5	17	12	7	19	10
5. Insuff.softw.	51	52	44	45	36	52	49	65	39	30
6. Softw. difficult	6	6	4	5	6	8	4	7	6	3
7. Softw. not adapt.	19	6	27	5	13	26	17	15	12	17
8. Poor qual. manuals	6	4	6	14	8	9	13	23	17	6
9. Lack info. softw.	13	13	18	15	10	14	27	17	12	7
10. Softw.not instruct.lang.	13	3	1	4	18	3	1	5	10	0
11. Not enough superv.	6	10	6	5	8	18	3	3	6	11
12. Integr. instruc.	9	17	14	39	17	7	13	12	12	17
13. Integr. curric.	25	15	17	29	9	11	9	7	12	13
14. Inappr.stud. age	0	0	1	2	1	1	2	3	0	0
15. Teachers lack knowledge	9	13	14	21	17	26	15	35	7	22
16. Insuff. exp. help	8	7	14	6	23	10	9	28	6	6
17. Insuff. time learn about	19	6	30	20	40	19	7	10	12	6
18. Computer location	9	24	13	17	8	9	8	8	4	21
19. Techn. operat.ass.	2	8	7	13	11	10	9	12	2	4
20. Comp. outside school	0	0	1	3	1	1	0	0	0	0
21. Schedule time	11	34	29	19	15	22	33	8	19	25
22. Access teachers	6	18	7	6	5	7	12	18	3	9
23. Insuf. training	11	8	12	1	41	34	19	25	8	13
24. No admin. support	2	0	4	1	12	7	3	0	4	4
25. Inadeq.fin. supp.	9	25	9	10	29	19	22	17	4	24
26. No fit school pol.	-	-	-	-	-	-	-	-	-	-
27. Time develop less.	26	44	30	45	40	51	53	45	26	35
28. Teach. innov. exper.	-	-	-	-	-	-	-	-	-	-
29. Teach. lack inter.	8	6	9	5	9	14	5	12	6	9

Notes. -: data not collected, countries with less than 50 cases not included.

Table D.12
Percentage principals in elementary schools including a reason in their top five selection of reasons for not using computers

Country / Educational System

	BFR	ISR	JPN	NET	POR
1. Insuff. computers	22	37	14	49	16
2. Insuff. periph.	5	7	2	5	2
3. Diffic. mainten.	0	3	7	1	0
4. Limitations comp.	-	-	-	-	-
5. Insuff.softw.	11	18	14	31	9
6. Softw. difficult	0	0	4	4	0
7. Softw. not adapt.	9	5	3	9	0
8. Poor qual. manuals	1	0	0	0	0
9. Lack info. softw.	18	10	10	5	7
10. Softw.not instruct.lang.	1	9	0	1	1
11. Not enough superv.	22	8	16	16	2
12. Integr. instruc.	20	4	8	15	10
13. Integr. curric.	4	4	5	7	7
14. Inappr.stud. age	0	0	0	0	0
15. Teachers lack knowledge	76	38	68	53	38
16. Insuff. exp. help	23	20	11	14	36
17. Insuff. time learn about	9	16	15	3	17
18. Computer location	31	23	13	31	29
19. Techn. operat.ass.	13	5	27	9	3
20. Comp. outside school	12	1	37	3	1
21. Schedule time	6	7	5	1	7
22. Access teachers	5	3	34	3	9
23. Insuf. training	26	9	44	9	48
24. No admin. support	13	25	33	15	17
25. Inadeq.fin. supp.	61	64	56	60	71
26. No fit school pol.	5	1	0	3	43
27. Time develop less.	10	5	19	22	4
28. Teach. innov. exper.	6	1	0	6	0
29. Teach. lack inter.	33	11	17	13	6

Notes. -: data not collected, countries with less than 50 cases not included.

Table D.13
*Percentage principals in lower secondary schools including a reason in
their top five selection of reasons for not using computers*

Country / Educational System

	BFL	GRE	JPN	POR	SWI
1. Insuff. computers	34	49	21	31	34
2. Insuff. periph.	11	8	3	6	3
3. Diffic. mainten.	0	1	10	0	1
4. Limitations comp.	-	-	-	-	-
5. Insuff.softw.	14	16	11	11	5
6. Softw. difficult	2	1	1	0	6
7. Softw. not adapt.	9	3	0	3	4
8. Poor qual. manuals	0	4	1	0	0
9. Lack info. softw.	4	4	6	9	2
10. Softw.not instruct.lang.	2	0	0	4	0
11. Not enough superv.	3	3	26	14	2
12. Integr. instruc.	29	12	5	16	13
13. Integr. curric.	37	14	10	4	15
14. Inappr.stud. age	6	0	7	0	6
15. Teachers lack knowledge	49	52	63	42	54
16. Insuff. exp. help	12	38	14	39	15
17. Insuff. time learn about	42	25	7	10	18
18. Computer location	24	31	12	22	26
19. Techn. operat.ass.	11	13	29	6	3
20. Comp. outside school	3	1	38	1	8
21. Schedule time	1	1	1	6	9
22. Access teachers	0	18	44	8	2
23. Insuf. training	9	39	56	43	6
24. No admin. support	7	22	41	25	9
25. Inadeq.fin. supp.	38	36	57	80	26
26. No fit school pol.	0	6	0	24	14
27. Time develop less.	9	11	8	5	11
28. Teach. innov. exper.	1	3	3	0	4
29. Teach. lack inter.	24	4	12	6	20

Notes. -: data not collected, countries with less than 50 cases not included.

Table D.14
Percentage principals in upper secondary schools including a reason in their top five selection of reasons for not using computers

Country / Educational System

	CHI	GRE	IND	POL
1. Insuff. computers	65	31	30	41
2. Insuff. periph.	26	4	3	2
3. Diffic. mainten.	3	3	23	14
4. Limitations comp.	-	-	-	-
5. Insuff.softw.	33	10	22	20
6. Softw. difficult	0	0	2	0
7. Softw. not adapt.	0	1	4	3
8. Poor qual. manuals	0	1	5	8
9. Lack info. softw.	0	9	19	13
10. Softw.not instruct.lang.	0	1	12	1
11. Not enough superv.	1	10	16	5
12. Integr. instruc.	14	13	10	13
13. Integr. curric.	5	25	8	0
14. Inappr.stud. age	0	0	2	0
15. Teachers lack knowledge	27	51	25	47
16. Insuff. exp. help	14	32	28	14
17. Insuff. time learn about	4	43	31	25
18. Computer location	13	33	23	32
19. Techn. operat.ass.	9	6	13	18
20. Comp. outside school	0	0	6	2
21. Schedule time	3	2	2	3
22. Access teachers	1	17	6	10
23. Insuf. training	30	28	28	12
24. No admin. support	26	24	20	13
25. Inadeq.fin. supp.	80	46	50	60
26. No fit school pol.	1	9	3	1
27. Time develop less.	6	10	17	11
28. Teach. innov. exper.	0	3	0	5
29. Teach. lack inter.	4	3	12	23

Notes. -: data not collected, countries with less than 50 cases not included.

Table D.15
*Percentage teachers in elementary schools including a reason in their
top five selection of reasons for not using computers*

Country / Educational System

	BFR	JPNNWZ		USA
1. Insuff. computers	42	43	72	53
2. Insuff. periph.	6	7	18	7
3. Diffic. mainten.	1	0	8	1
4. Limitations comp.	2	0	4	3
5. Insuff.softw.	16	0	22	14
6. Softw. difficult	1	0	4	3
7. Softw. not adapt.	3	0	0	9
8. Poor qual. manuals	0	0	0	1
9. Lack info. softw.	17	0	10	7
10. Softw.not instruct.lang.	1	82	0	0
11. Not enough superv.	14	18	12	32
12. Integr. instruc.	14	19	16	43
13. Integr. curric.	14	0	2	12
14. Inappr.stud. age	1	0	0	1
15. Teachers lack knowledge	66	0	62	57
16. Insuff. exp. help	25	0	30	11
17. Insuff. time learn about	16	0	8	20
18. Computer location	19	0	14	17
19. Techn. operat.ass.	5	0	12	10
20. Comp. outside school	8	79	6	1
21. Schedule time	13	8	22	26
22. Access teachers	8	26	8	21
23. Insuf. training	30	0	38	18
24. No admin. support	12	0	10	7
25. Inadeq.fin. supp.	28	0	16	10
26. No fit school pol.	8	0	2	0
27. Time develop less.	25	0	10	32
28. Teach. innov. exper.	2	0	0	0
29. Teach. lack inter.	12	0	2	1

Notes. -: data not collected, countries with less than 50 cases not included.

Table D.16
Percentage existing subjects teachers in lower secondary schools including a reason in their top five selection of reasons for not using computers

Country / Educational System

	BFL	BFR	CBC	FRA	FRG	GRE	JPN	LUX	NET	NWZ	POR	SWI	USA
1. Insuff. computers	28	37	50	31	17	61	45	33	25	39	43	28	41
2. Insuff. periph.	5	4	7	4	3	4	10	0	2	6	1	5	7
3. Diffic. mainten.	1	2	1	8	1	0	6	0	3	3	0	1	2
4. Limitations comp.	2	2	1	6	3	2	3	2	3	3	1	4	6
5. Insuff.softw.	17	16	35	23	13	17	38	11	44	31	26	31	24
6. Softw. difficult	3	3	2	2	3	1	11	2	8	6	0	6	2
7. Softw. not adapt.	16	7	9	16	1	4	8	13	15	10	7	12	9
8. Poor qual. manuals	4	2	1	1	1	2	2	0	2	4	6	3	2
9. Lack info. softw.	13	23	24	21	10	13	12	7	10	21	20	14	12
10. Softw.not instruct.lang.	2	1	3	0	0	8	1	4	1	1	3	2	0
11. Not enough superv.	6	8	5	18	1	4	13	9	9	8	7	4	16
12. Integr. instruc.	22	28	18	30	27	13	21	40	20	21	19	26	33
13. Integr. curric.	23	30	18	21	24	14	13	40	25	12	21	26	16
14. Inappr.stud. age	3	6	2	1	4	0	2	5	1	1	0	3	1
15. Teachers lack knowledge	50	63	43	40	53	45	56	58	35	56	56	54	50
16. Insuff. exp. help	30	26	17	18	13	47	14	22	16	27	40	14	15
17. Insuff. time learn about	34	28	13	28	25	21	22	24	29	19	47	20	17
18. Computer location	10	14	15	7	4	6	13	9	9	10	6	7	16
19. Techn. operat.ass.	3	2	1	5	5	4	11	2	3	5	0	1	7
20. Comp. outside school	1	1	0	0	2	3	9	4	2	1	4	7	1
21. Schedule time	8	24	26	38	10	0	9	20	12	35	7	8	28
22. Access teachers	4	7	17	4	6	12	15	9	5	12	3	2	22
23. Insuf. training	22	17	23	20	9	24	40	22	13	36	29	11	21
24. No admin. support	3	6	4	1	5	2	6	4	2	9	17	3	3
25. Inadeq.fin. supp.	6	7	13	1	5	12	22	5	9	6	16	2	13
26. No fit school pol.	1	1	0	1	0	5	2	0	0	1	10	15	0
27. Time develop less.	33	43	35	31	12	11	38	20	46	46	19	24	35
28. Teach. innov. exper.	3	2	1	1	2	0	0	0	2	1	0	1	0
29. Teach. lack inter.	16	3	1	4	5	3	4	4	7	1	3	2	3

Notes. -: data not collected, countries with less than 50 cases not included.

Table D.17
Percentage existing subjects teachers in upper secondary schools including a reason in their top five selection of reasons for not using computers

Country / Educational System

	BFL	BFR	CBC	FRA	FRG	GRE	HUN	IND	ISR	JPN	NWZ	POL	POR	SLO	SWI	USA
1. Insuff. computers	21	25	57	23	17	30	32	44	28	32	26	40	40	34	23	46
2. Insuff. periph.	2	3	14	8	2	3	8	5	8	5	6	10	8	10	4	6
3. Diffic. mainten.	1	1	0	4	2	2	0	10	2	4	1	9	0	2	1	1
4. Limitations comp.	4	4	6	9	7	0	4	4	11	3	5	3	3	5	3	6
5. Insuff.softw.	24	15	38	18	25	13	31	35	47	44	27	32	24	23	23	33
6. Softw. difficult	4	1	2	2	3	0	6	3	1	9	4	7	0	3	5	1
7. Softw. not adapt.	22	8	23	19	2	14	9	10	25	16	17	13	13	13	12	13
8. Poor qual. manuals	3	2	6	3	1	0	12	7	2	3	3	27	5	2	2	3
9. Lack info. softw.	11	23	23	18	12	24	15	17	29	14	30	17	19	13	12	12
10. Softw.not instruct.lang.	3	2	4	1	0	12	2	13	7	2	2	3	5	3	4	0
11. Not enough superv.	1	2	3	8	2	3	3	13	6	15	4	2	3	10	2	13
12. Integr. instruc.	32	28	27	29	18	28	44	17	16	26	28	14	21	19	26	32
13. Integr. curric.	40	37	30	35	40	27	31	10	16	20	17	7	19	26	32	22
14. Inappr.stud. age	1	0	1	0	4	0	2	1	2	1	1	1	0	2	3	3
15. Teachers lack knowledge	38	58	28	42	41	61	63	40	42	54	52	61	60	61	39	58
16. Insuff. exp. help	21	25	19	17	10	57	11	25	38	16	19	35	35	27	15	14
17. Insuff. time learn about	39	19	4	33	40	42	27	33	26	28	7	18	35	15	15	6
18. Computer location	8	6	19	10	1	6	14	4	3	10	10	10	16	21	5	20
19. Techn. operat.ass.	3	1	2	3	1	0	11	10	3	8	2	5	0	3	0	3
20. Comp. outside school	1	0	0	0	0	1	0	2	3	1	1	0	2	5	2	0
21. Schedule time	10	26	31	34	19	9	14	14	12	18	25	3	13	13	17	22
22. Access teachers	4	10	13	10	3	19	5	13	12	12	10	15	11	19	3	25
23. Insuf. training	11	15	19	18	4	38	12	39	16	36	30	22	38	11	7	26
24. No admin. support	3	2	3	2	2	4	1	13	5	8	2	1	10	6	2	6
25. Inadeq.fin. supp.	6	3	18	4	5	17	4	15	10	14	12	10	11	15	2	22
26. No fit school pol.	0	2	1	0	0	10	0	8	4	5	0	0	8	2	16	0
27. Time develop less.	32	38	31	30	17	12	30	35	19	43	40	39	21	24	30	44
28. Teach. innov. exper.	2	2	0	1	0	0	0	1	1	1	0	1	0	3	0	0
29. Teach. lack inter.	11	1	3	1	2	1	1	9	4	6	1	2	2	6	2	1

Notes. -: data not collected, countries with less than 50 cases not included.

Appendix E

Results of LISREL analyses for the USA and
the Netherlands

Measuring and Predicting Computer Implementation in Dutch and United States Schools: A Structural Model

Purpose and analytical approach

As was suggested previously in this report, the implementation strategies adopted by educational authorities and schools do not seem to take into account sufficiently the interrelatedness of factors that are necessary for the successful introduction of computers in schools. The purpose of the analyses of data reported in this appendix is to investigate the factors that may explain why certain schools have developed active innovation strategies for implementing computer education and, secondly, why some schools are using computers for educative purposes to a greater extent than others.

The approach taken in estimating the relationships existing among the factors determining the degree of computer implementation in schools is to develop a structural model in which the magnitude of the hypothesized relationships can be approximated and their statistical significance assessed. Not all factors known from previous research studies to co-vary with indicators of computer use in school education can be specified meaningfully in such a model. It is indeed inevitable that the holistic perspective implicit in the approach adopted in previous chapters is given up, as simplification and data reduction are essential elements in an analytical strategy aimed at causal explanation. The purpose of the analysis of data is ultimately to provide decision-makers and school personnel faced with the challenge of improving the quality of computer education with useful, policy-relevant information. Hence the study is principally focussed on variables alterable by policy intervention.

Previous research

The findings of previous research studies, including those elaborated in the present volume, seem to suggest that the extent to which computers are successfully introduced in school education is enhanced by different situational, financial, organizational and dispositional factors (see, e.g., Becker, 1983; Kulik *et al.*, 1983; Van den Akker *et al.*, 1991).

Lists of factors that possibly influence innovation implementation in education are proposed by Fullan (1982, 1985), Van Velzen *et al.* (1985), Pelgrum and Plomp (1988), Van den Berg *et al.* (1989). These authors generally distinguish between different sets of explanatory variables. However, so far there have been few attempts, if any, to order these antecedent variables, and their relationships with computer implementation in schools, in a conceptual sequence. At least three sets of predictor variables are commonly mentioned in the research literature: system-level variables and measures of external support, indicators of school organization and classroom practice, and characteristics of the innovation.

System-level variables include specific policy variables, such as rules and prescriptions with respect to curriculum content and the use of teaching methods and differentiation. External support for the innovation is commonly indexed by variables measuring financial aid and other aspects of logistical support for the innovation provided by government agencies and business enterprises. External support is also conceptualized in nonmaterial terms, for example, assistance with respect to inservice teacher training, internal staff development, coaching and guidance of individual teachers and the facilitation of personal contacts with experts and colleagues from other schools.

A large number of school-level variables are known from previous research on school effectiveness to co-vary with the successful implementation of an educational innovation (e.g. Reynolds and Walberg, 1989; Creemers and Scheerens, eds, 1989). Important among these are indicators of school size, type and area location, composition of the student body, school management style, leadership characteristics, general teacher competence and their readiness for accepting the innovation, the availability of facilities and innovation-specific equipment, and experiences gained previously in implementing an educational innovation.

Innovation characteristics are commonly assessed using measures of the explicitness, clarity and practicality of innovation relevant aspects of school policy and staff development policy. Other characteristics include the perceptions by the school leader and staff of the relevance of the innovation and their belief in the worthwhileness of eventual outcomes. Moreover, the strategy of implementation adopted by the school as a result of policy commitment and measures of specific outcomes of the innovation are also of interest.

Structural model

A causal structure can be hypothesized between the factors mentioned above. In Figure 1 a hypothesized path model is shown in which important determinants of computer implementation width are specified. The conceptual sequence determining the ordering of variables in this recursive path model is based on the conceptual framework presented in Chapter 1. However, it must be noted at the outset that not all theoretically relevant variables are incorporated. As was mentioned before, the present analysis is principally aimed at identifying and modelling the substantial effects of possibly manipulative antecedent factors on computer implementation in Dutch and U.S. schools. Hence the decision to specify a particular construct in the model was influenced by theoretical considerations, the results obtained in previous research, and currently available data.

The product moment correlations estimated among the many items collected for the IEA study of computers in education were examined prior to model specification. The aim was to arrive at a relatively small number of meaningful and possibly alterable antecedent factors. Data reduction took place also for other reasons. Firstly, system-level explanatory factors could not be included because only two systems were studied. Secondly, the method used to fit the model to the data could not appropriately handle multilevel relationships. Hence teacher level data could not be utilized at the present stage in the analysis. Thirdly, several relevant constructs had to be dropped because adequate identification could not be achieved. This was due either to general data insufficiency or specific measurement problems. Figure 1 shows the resulting structural model.

Target population and sample

Each path indicated in the diagram denotes a hypothesized relationship. These hypotheses are tested empirically using data derived from a population of schools sampled in the Netherlands and the United States. The data were collected early in 1989. All lower secondary schools providing an education for students in the grade in which the modal age is 13 years constitute the target population from which the nationally representative samples of schools were drawn.

For obvious reasons, the data sets examined in this appendix had to be restricted to schools actually using computers for instructional purposes. The number of schools in the Dutch data set after such restriction had taken place was too small to warrant the use of the LISREL method.

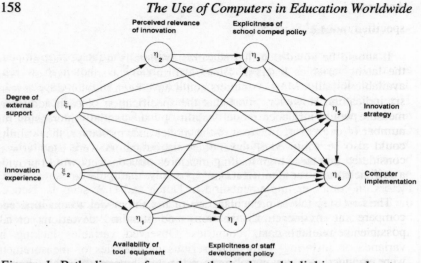

Figure 1. Path diagram for a hypothesized model linking explanatory factors to the implementation of computers in school education.

Given the diversified strcture of the Dutch educational system, 141 upper secondary schools could justifiably be added to the sampled data set. It must be noted that this procedure resulted in decreased standard error values and improved stability, but did not alter the structure of the relationships in the Dutch model. In all, a total of 368 Dutch schools was examined, compared with 397 schools in the United States.

Variables

The mean scores and standard deviations of the manifest or observed variables are presented in Table 1. The information used to measure these variables was taken from the questionnaire instruments to which the school principals and resource persons acting as computer coordinator had responded. The latent variables underlying the different items are also mentioned. Furthermore, the loadings of the manifest variables in measuring their construct are indicated. These loadings were obtained with the use of the linear structural relations (LISREL) approach and the maximum likelihood method (Jöreskog and Sörbom, 1990). The squared factor loadings shown in Table 1 can be interpreted as lower bound estimates of the reliability of the measures making up the constructs. It can be seen that the reliability of the measures included in the Dutch model are generally not as substantial as the measures specified in the U.S. model.

It should be noted that the measures eventually used as indicators of the latent variables listed in Table 1 form only a small part of those available initially. Most constructs could have been measured by at least six indicators. However, given that the specification of each additional measure would influence model stability by substantially increasing the number of degrees of freedom in the model and, moreover, that validity could also be achieved if fewer than six indicators were used, it was considered that three high loading measures per construct would provide a sufficient basis for identification.

The first step taken in the selection of indicators was to examine and compare the frequency distributions and standard deviations of all possible items across six countries. Observed variables lacking in variance or suffering from other serious deficiencies of measurement were excluded. An attempt to improve the distributions of highly skewed variables was made early in the study, by applying transformation procedures. The aim was to achieve as closely as possible a normal distribution of scores across categories. Another aim was to recode all measures in a positive direction. The method of principal components analysis was used to select and exclude manifest variables with confounded measurements. Data reduction occurred also at a later stage, when congeneric factor scores were estimated in order to identify and delete variables with insufficient reliability or high multicollinearity. Finally, if a given item had not been collected in at least two of the six countries initially studied in this analysis, then the variable was excluded from further study.

It can be inferred from Table 1 that the two models deviate in a few minor respects, despite all efforts taken to ensure full comparability. However, it should also be noted that the measurement models may be considered very close to this ideal, as at least two of each three indicators are identical and, also, because only the common measures are employed in assigning scale values to latent variables.

Table 1
Description and summary statistics of latent constructs and their associated manifest variables

Latent construct	United States				Netherlands			
Manifest variable	Mean	S.D.	R^2_a	λ_b	Mean	S.D.	R^2	λ_b
Y_6 Computer Implementation								
Total grades and subjects with computer use	2.01	0.69	0.43	0.65	2.10	0.55	0.82	0.91
Instruction in computers in school subjects	2.96	1.14	0.25	0.49	2.30	0.64	n.a.	n.a.
Number of teachers using computers	2.02	0.80	0.39	0.61	1.96	0.76	0.39	0.62
Y_5 Active Innovation Strategy								
Active assessment of computer use	2.11	0.76	0.46	0.66	2.02	0.44	0.50	0.70
Internal computer use info exchange	2.38	0.79	0.76	0.87	2.12	0.58	0.58	0.76
External computer use info exchange	2.15	0.65	0.38	0.60	1.81	0.48	0.27	0.52
Y_4 Staff Development Policy								
Give introductory course on computer use	1.16	0.37	0.54	0.73	n.a.	n.a.	n.a.	n.a.
Using computer application programs	1.20	0.40	0.67	0.82	1.54	0.50	0.35	0.60
Using computers in specific school subjects	1.17	0.37	0.50	0.70	1.25	0.43	0.46	0.68
Give computer science course	n.a.	n.a.	n.a.	n.a.	1.41	0.49	0.69	0.83
Y_3 School Computer Education Policy								
Assign priorities on instruction use	1.12	0.32	0.27	0.52	1.67	0.47	0.43	0.66
Define goals for instruction with computers	1.11	0.31	0.46	0.68	1.70	0.46	0.22	0.47
Prescribe computer use in grades	1.15	0.36	0.23	0.49	1.64	0.48	0.34	0.58
Y_2 Perceived Relevance[c]								
Computers help teach more effectively	2.04	0.66	0.66	0.80	1.56	0.50	0.17	0.41
Computers enhance students' creativity	2.12	0.67	0.57	0.75	n.a.	n.a.	n.a.	n.a.
Computers lead to more productivity	n.a.	n.a.	n.a.	n.a.	1.29	0.46	0.73	0.86
Computers increase student achievement	2.21	0.64	0.91	0.95	1.33	0.47	0.51	0.71
Y_1 Availability Tool Equipment								
Sufficient powerful computers	1.87	1.03	0.59	0.77	1.84	1.01	0.78	0.89
Network for shared disk storage	1.81	1.01	0.39	0.62	1.96	1.04	0.31	0.56
Sufficient tool software	n.a.	n.a.	n.a.	n.a.	2.58	0.99	0.09	0.30
Sufficient variety of software	2.87	0.96	0.23	0.47	n.a.	n.a.	n.a.	n.a.
X_2 Innovation Experience[d]								
Length of period of computer use	2.87	1.13	0.54	0.73	2.00	0.77	0.63	0.79
X_1 External Support[e]								
External support for innovation (8 items)	1.38	0.49	0.78	0.88	1.67	0.47	0.63	0.79

Notes. [a] this statistic, the explained variance in the indicator, may be interpreted as an estimate of the reliability of the indicator in measuring the latent construct. [b] $\lambda=$ factor loading. [c] The items constituting perceived relevance are measured on a three-category scale in the U.S. data set and on a two-category scale in the case of the Netherlands. [d] The reliablity estimate and factor loading were estimated in a multiple item congeneric test model. [e] The reliability estimate was estimated using a scale reliability analysis procedure (Cronbach α). Included items involved support from development institutes and resource centers in the following areas: financial, expertise, teacher training and other instructional.

Naturally, some case loss was encountered in the IEA study of computers in school education. The presence of missing observations is discussed in the previous chapters. Research workers generally acknowledge the possibility of contamination in elicited responses as a result of missing data (Kish, 1987; Rubin, 1987). This situation poses several problems of a conceptual and analytical nature. For example, in order to obtain accurate estimates of standard errors and indicators of the "goodness" of model fit using conventional statistical tests, a simple random sample design is commonly assumed and full data coverage on all measures required. A multistage procedure of compensation for missing data was therefore used. The records of schools were singled out in the first step and eventual gaps were filled-in using auxiliary data. If imputation was not possible, for example because relevant auxiliary data were not available, then variable grand mean scores were inserted for missing data in a second step. Data sets with full coverage on all measures were built up in this way.

It can be seen from Table 1 that the dependent variable, computer education implementation was measured using three indicators. The first is a measure of the number of different subject teachers using computers. Whereas the second measures the number of subjects in which students receive computer education, the third refers to the number of grades in which teachers employ computers for educational purposes.

Method

Even though an attempt was made to improve the distributional properties of ordinal variables, entirely normal distributions of scores on categories were not achieved in all cases. Moreover, several items were measured on dichotomous scales. Matrices of polychoric and polyserial correlation coefficients were therefore employed instead of product moment correlations. The method of linear structural relations analysis (LISREL) and the maximum likelihood approach were employed in the fitting of the model to the data. As can be seen from the reliability estimates presented in Table 1, most items were measured with substantial error. The LISREL method was used in this study because it could take the possibly biasing effects of measurement errors and residual covariances into account. The assumptions guiding the use of LISREL are described in detail by Jöreskog and Sörbom (1990).

Results: The U.S. Case

An over-identified recursive path model is presented in Figure 2. It shows the results obtained in the fitting of the U.S. data set to the model. Each path represents a statistically significant standardized regression relationship. Hence paths not shown failed to reach the five per cent threshold level of significance. It may be noted that the "goodness" of fit of the data to the model is adequate if the probability value of 0.10 is used as the threshold for accepting the fit of the model, as has become standard practice. Different indicators of the fit of the data to the model are given in Table I in the supplement. It can be seen here that the over-identified model, with 12 fitted residuals, has 148 degrees of freedom and an overall χ^2 estimate of 162, which corresponds to a probability value of 0.21.

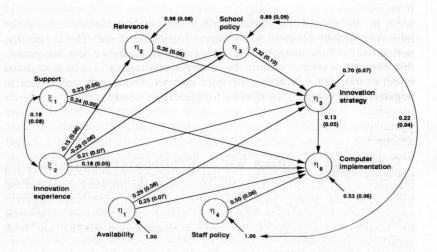

Figure 2. Standardized effects on innovation strategy and computer implementation, U.S. school data (standard errors in parentheses).

The following are the substantive findings with respect to the implementation of computer education in U.S. lower secondary schools. First, the variable external support exerts a direct, significant effect on school computer education policy (0.23) and implementation (0.24). It may be a surprise to some readers to find that support does not influence availability. The explanation is that the variables used in measuring the construct are concerned mostly with the technical and expertise support provided by resource centers. Business support was specified in another path model, which is not shown here because its adequacy in terms of fit was too poor. In this model, business support was found to exert strong positive effects on availability, school policy, and staff development policy.

Innovation experience, which is a measure of the number of years of experience schools have with respect to the provision of computer education, influences negatively both perceived relevance of the innovation and the innovation strategy handled by the school. At first sight, these findings may seem surprising. However, it can be recalled from the results presented in previous chapters that the United States is among the few countries in which computers were introduced into schools at an early stage. Computers were being used in 86 per cent of all lower secondary schools in the United States by 1985. The negative path from innovation history to the benefits of computer use in schools would seem to suggest that the more recently computers were introduced, the more favourable the perception of the school principal. The longer the period over which computers have been in actual use, the less favourable this perception on the part of the leadership becomes. The standardized effect of innovation history on school computer education policy is also negative in direction. This may be interpreted as showing that the schools in which computers were introduced just recently tend to have formulated an explicit school policy, more than is apparently the case among the schools in which computers have been present for a longer time period. A related explanation may be that policy is drawn up explicitly in order to facilitate the introduction of an innovation, and that it becomes less important, or is forgotten, once the implementation of the innovation has gotten underway. The results provide some indirect support for this hypothesis because the effects of innovation experience on innovation strategy (0.21) and implementation (0.18) are both significant and positive.

As expected, substantial effects on innovation strategy are estimated for perceived relevance (0.35), availability of tool equipment (0.29), and school computer education policy (0.32). Availability exerts, moreover, a direct influence on computer education implementation. Staff development policy exerts a particularly strong effect on implementation (0.50). The correlation between school computer policy and staff development policy is also significant. Finally, innovation strategy is found to influence significantly, although weakly, implementation.

Supplementary Table II presents estimates of the amount of variance explained by the antecedent variables in the latent variables. It can be seen that the first four dependent variables are not predicted adequately, as the standard errors are large relative to the values of the estimates. This is not the case with respect to the explanation of the two criterion variables, innovation strategy and degree of actual implementation. Thirty per cent of the variance in innovation strategy is explained by the four antecedent factors. Significant effects on implementation are found for five antecedents. Collectively they account for 47 per cent of the variance in implementation.

On the whole, most relationships hypothesized in Figure 1 are supported by the results. Some hypotheses are rejected, however. One example is the hypothesized effect of external support on perceived relevance (1) and availability (2). Another is the effect of innovation history on availability (3), and of the latter on staff development policy (4). It can be concluded safely that more research on the definition and measurement of the constructs is required.

Results: The Netherlands

What has been said in the preceding paragraphs about the structure and overall fit of the U.S. model applies equally well in the Dutch case. The substantive results are indicated in the path model in Figure 3. The effects of external support are of interest. Whereas the direction of the effect on implementation is positive in direction (0.24), this is not the case with respect to the influence on availability (-0.28). It would thus seem that measures taken to improve teacher competence may be expected to also have an impact on computer use. As a consequence, the demand for computer equipment and facilities is likely to increase. This can be inferred from the finding that external support exerts a negative effect on availability, particularly because the latter construct reflects the perception of respondents with respect to the sufficiency of the available computers.

It can be concluded on the basis of the positive, significant values estimated for the effects of innovation experience on availability (0.19) and innovation strategy (0.31) that schools tend to acquire more computers over time and, moreover, develop active strategies for the implementation of computers in education. These strategies are influenced also by perceptions of the relevance and benefits of the innovation. Another factor of importance in this regard is whether schools have formulated policy.

As can be seen from figure 3, the length of computer use appears to be negatively correlated with the variable external support. This may well mean that schools with many years of computer experience have started on their own, while schools in which computers were recently introduced have received external support.

As was discussed previously in this report, computers have been introduced and integrated in school education in the Netherlands to a limited extent, at least by comparison with some other countries, and notably the U.S. This observation is further qualified by the finding reported in supplementary Table II, that a relatively small part of the variance in implementation width (0.12) is explained in the Dutch model. Three significant effects on implementation are found, namely, staff development policy (0.21), external support (0.24), and active innovation strategy (0.13). Even though these effects are worthwhile, the results indicate that there must be a number of additional factors influencing the successful introduction of computer education in Dutch schools. The results also suggest that the emphasis in the Netherlands at present is on the formulation of specific school policy and the development of an active strategy for introducing the innovation. The following can therefore be hypothesized: if a similar research study were carried out a few years hence, then an increased amount of variance in implementation width will be explained.

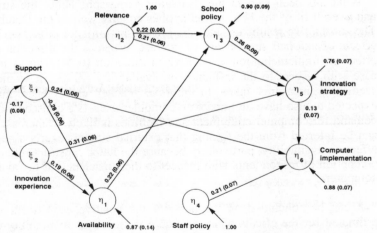

Figure 3. Standardized effects on innovation strategy and computer implementation, Dutch school data (standard errors in parentheses).

Comparison

The first striking difference is that there are fewer significant effect relationships in the Dutch model compared with the U.S. one. This is also reflected in the correlations recorded in Table III in the supplement. A second point is that there are clear differences between the two countries with respect to both the nature and the magnitude of the effects on the two dependent variables, active innovation strategy and computer education implementation.

Table 2 presents estimates of the total and indirect effects of the antecedent variables on active innovation strategy. The standard errors of the estimates are also provided. School computer education policy is the most powerful predictor of innovation strategy in both the United States (0.41) and the Netherlands (0.30). Innovation experience and perceived relevance have significant effects on active innovation strategy in both countries. The low value associated with the influence of innovation experience in the United States model is due to an indirect negative effect mediated by perceived relevance and school policy. On the whole, the results obtained in the determination of active innovation strategy are similar in both countries.

Table 2
Indirect and total effects on active innovation strategy (standard errors in parentheses)

| Predictor Variables | Dependent Variable: Active Innovation Strategy | | | |
| | U.S. Schools ($R^2 = 0.30$) | | Dutch Schools ($R^2 = 0.24$) | |
	Indirect Effect	Total Effect	Indirect Effect	Total Effect
X_1 External Support	0.06 (0.02)	0.06 (0.02)	- 0.01 (0.01)	- 0.01 (0.01)
X_2 Innovation Experience	- 0.13 (0.04)	0.06 (0.06)	0.01 (0.00)	0.24 (0.06)
Y_1 Availability Tool Equipment	n.a.	0.33 (0.08)	0.05 (0.02)	0.05 (0.02)
Y_2 Perceived Relevance	n.a.	0.32 (0.05)	0.05 (0.02)	0.23 (0.06)
Y_3 School Computer Policy	n.a.	0.41 (0.10)	n.a.	0.30 (0.09)
Y_4 Staff Development Policy	n.a.	n.a.	n.a.	n.a.

Notes. (a) Effect relationships are estimated using the maximum likelihood fit function. (b) Underlined coefficients are *not* significant at the five per cent level. (c) All other coefficients are statistically significant, at least at the five per cent level. (d) The unstandardized direct effect can be inferred from the data recorded in this table, as TE = DE + IE.

Table 3

Indirect and total effects on degree of computer implemention

	Dependent Variable: Degree of Computer Implementation						
	U.S. Schools ($R^2 = 0.47$)				Dutch Schools ($R^2 = 0.12$)		
Predictor Variables	Indirect Effect		Total Effect		Indirect Effect		Total Effect	
X_1 External Support	<u>0.01</u>	(0.02)	0.16	(0.05)	<u>0.00</u>		0.21	(0.06)
X_2 Innovation Experience	<u>0.01</u>	(0.01)	0.13	(0.05)	0.04	(0.02)	0.04	(0.02)
Y_1 Availability Equipment	<u>0.03</u>	(0.02)	0.25	(0.06)	<u>0.01</u>	(0.01)	0.01	(0.01)
Y_2 Perceived Relevance	0.04	(0.02)	0.04	(0.02)	0.04	(0.02)	0.04	(0.02)
Y_3 School Computer Policy	0.04	(0.02)	0.04	(0.02)	0.06	(0.03)	0.06	(0.03)
Y_4 Staff Development Policy	n.a.		0.40	(0.06)	n.a.		0.23	(0.07)
Y_5 Innovation Strategy	n.a.		0.10	(0.05)	n.a.		0.15	(0.08)

Notes. (a) Effect relationships are estimated using the maximum likelihood fit function. (b) Underlined coefficients are *not* significant at the five per cent level. (c) All other coefficients are statistically significant, at least at the five per cent level. (d) The unstandardized direct effect can be inferred from the data recorded in this table, as TE = DE + IE.

Table 3 presents estimates of the total and indirect effects on computer implementation. It must be noted at the outset that the value of the coefficient of determination (0.12) obtained in the Dutch model is in doubt. As can be seen from supplementary Table II, the standard error of this estimate is 0.07. Hence it must be concluded that the antecedent variables failed in predicting adequately the dependent variable, computer implementation, in the case of the Netherlands. By contrast, nearly 50 per cent of the variance in this criterion could be accounted for in the model of the United States. The difference arises in part because the effects on implementation of innovation experience and availability are substantial in the United States but not in the Netherlands, and also because the influence of staff development policy is more substantial in the United States.

The results presented above would seem to indicate that the system of education in the United States is ahead of the Dutch system in implementing computers in schools. The outcome variable, implementation, can be adequately predicted in the former system. By contrast, in the case of the Netherlands, the predictive capacity of the model is directed towards the explanation of mediating variables, such as the development of school policy and the design of an active implementation strategy.

Implications for Future Research

Even though a confirmatory factor analytic procedure was employed in this study in estimating the structural relationships among the productive factors, the findings must nevertheless be considered tentative. There are several reasons for this. Firstly, the dependent variable in the model, computer implementation, was measured at the between-school and not the between-classroom level. This will be one of the aims of the second stage of the IEA computers in education study. Secondly, it was found in the process of model building that the construct, teacher expertise and readiness, could not be identified with the use of indirect measures based on the perceptions of teacher quality of the school principal and computer coordinator. Hence ways of measuring teacher competence directly and aggregating the data to school level have to be found. Thirdly, the model was fitted to data collected in only two educational systems. It may be of interest to test the hypotheses guiding the specification of variables in the model against data collected in additional systems. Such an elaboration would not only offer a means of examining the validity of the model and provide a context for interpreting the findings, but would also make it possible to test empirically the central hypothesis guiding the design of this comparative study, namely, that there are certain distinctive developmental stages through which all systems seeking to implement computers in schools proceed. Finally, it would be of great interest if the relationships of the productive antecedent factors in the U.S. and Dutch models, on the one hand, and measures of classroom practice and student achievement on the other, could be estimated. This information is indispensible, as it may well provide decision-makers and school personnel with the practical knowledge they require in order to improve the quality and effectiveness of computer use in education.

STATISTICAL SUPPLEMENT

Table I
Indicators of the degree of "goodness of fit" of alternative models to the two data sets

Stages in model building	United States Model				Dutch Model			
	D.f.	p.	χ^2	RMR	D.f.	p.	χ^2	RMR
1. Just-identified, fully recursive model with diagonally free error matrices	145	0.00	260.7	0.04	145	0.00	245.2	0.05
2. Just-identified, fully recursive model with fitted residuals	133	0.20	146.4	0.03	128	0.35	133.8	0.004
3. Reduced-form structural model with fitted residuals	148	0.21	161.8	0.04	145	0.44	147.0	0.04

Notes. (a) D.f. = degrees of freedom. (b) p. = probability value. (c) χ^2 = chi-square statistic. (d) RMR = root mean square residual.

Table II
Coefficients of determination (R^2) of dependent latent constructs (standard errors in parentheses)

Constructs	U.S. Model		Dutch Model	
Y_6 Degree of Implementation	0.47	(0.06)	0.12	(0.07)
Y_5 Active Innovation Strategy	0.30	(0.07)	0.24	(0.07)
Y_4 Staff Development Policy	0.00	(0.08)	0.00	(0.10)
Y_3 School Computer Policy	0.11	(0.09)	0.10	(0.09)
Y_2 Perceived Relevance of Innovation	0.02	(0.08)	0.00	(0.11)
Y_1 Availability of Tool Equipment	0.00	(0.10)	0.13	(0.14)

Notes. (a) the coefficient of determination denotes the amount (per cent) of variance explained by the predictor variables in the dependent variable. (b) Underlined coefficients are *not* significant at the five per cent threshold level.

Table III

Disattenuated correlations among latent constructs (U.S. schools below diagonal; Netherlands schools above diagonal)

Construct	X_1	X_2	Y_1	Y_2	Y_3	Y_4	Y_5	Y_6
X_1 External Support	1.00	-0.17	-0.31	<u>0.00</u>	-0.07	<u>0.00</u>	-0.07	0.23
X_2 Innovation Experience	0.18	1.00	0.23	<u>0.00</u>	0.05	<u>0.00</u>	0.32	<u>0.00</u>
Y_1 Availability Tool Equipment	<u>0.00</u>	<u>0.00</u>	1.00	<u>0.00</u>	0.22	<u>0.00</u>	0.13	-0.06
Y_2 Perceived Relevance	-0.03	-0.15	<u>0.00</u>	1.00	0.22	<u>0.00</u>	0.26	0.03
Y_3 School Computer Policy	0.18	-0.25	<u>0.00</u>	0.04	1.00	<u>0.00</u>	0.32	0.02
Y_4 Staff Development Policy	<u>0.00</u>	<u>0.00</u>	<u>0.00</u>	<u>0.00</u>	0.22	1.00	<u>0.00</u>	0.21
Y_5 Active Innovation Strategy	0.09	0.08	0.29	0.33	0.28	0.07	1.00	0.11
Y_6 Computer Implementation	0.28	0.24	0.29	0.01	0.14	0.50	0.28	1.00

Notes. (a) the correlations are estimated using the maximum likelihood fit function. Measurement errors and significant error covariances are taken into account. (b) Disattenuated correlations cannot be computed in case a dependent variable has not been determined in the model. This is the case with underlined values.

References

Akker, J. van den, Keursten, P. and Plomp, Tj. (1991). The Integration of Computers in Education. *International Journal of Educational Research*, in press.

Becker, H. J. (1983). *School Uses of Microcomputers. Reports of a National Survey.* Center for the Organization of Schools, Baltimore, M.D.: The John Hopkins University. Press.

Berg, R. van den., Hameyer, U. and Stokking K. (1989). *Dissemination Reconsidered: The Demands of Implementation.* Leuven: ACCO.

Creemers, B. P. M., Scheerens, J. (eds) (1989). Developments in School Effectiveness Research. *International Journal of Educational Research.* Oxford: Pergamon Press

Jöreskog, K. G. and Sörbom, D. (1990). Linear Structural Relations Analysis. In: Husén, T. and Postlethwaite, T. N. (eds), *The International Encyclopedia of Education, Supplementary Volume II,* pp. 368-376. Oxford: Pergamon Press.

Fullan, M. (1982). *The Meaning of Educational Change.* New York: Teachers College Press.

Fullan, M. (1985). Curriculum Implementation. In: Husén, T. and Postlethwaite, T. N. (eds), *The International Encyclopedia of Education.* (pp. 1208-1215). Oxford: Pergamon Press.

Kish, L. (1987). *Statistical Design for Research.* New York: Wiley

Kulik, J. A., Bangert, R. L. and Williams, G. W. (1983). Effects of Computer-based College Teaching. *Review of Educational Research,* 50, 525-544

Pelgrum, W. J. and Plomp, Tj. (1988). The IEA study "Computers in Education:" A Multi-national Longitudinal Assessment. In: F. Lovis and E. D. Tagg (eds), *Computers in Education* (pp. 433-437). Amsterdam: Elsevier Science Publishers.

Reynolds, A. J. and Walberg, H. J. (1990). *A Structural Model of Educational Productivity.* Unpublished manuscript. Chicago: University of Illinois at Chicago.

Rubin, D. B. (1987). *Multiple Imputation for Nonresponse in Surveys.* New York: Wiley.

Velzen, W. G. van., Miles, M. B., Ekholm, M., Hameyer, U. and Robin, D. (1985). *Making School Improvement Work: A Conceptual Guide to Practice.* Leuven: ACCO.

Appendix F

Reliabilities of attitude scales

Table F.1
Alpha reliabilities per educational system and category of respondents on attitude scales

Country/Educational System

Scales/Levels	BFR	CBC	FRA	ISR	JPN	NET	NWZ	POR	USA
Elementary Schools									
EDUCATIONAL IMPACT									
Principals									
Using	.75	.80	.84	.67	.89	.81	.77	.72	.80
Non-using	.85	m	m	.72	.87	.76	.88	.80	m
Total	.80	.80	.84	.69	.89	.79	.80	.78	.80
Teachers									
Using	.76	.87	.84	.81	.89	.74	.86	m	.86
Non-using	.88	m	m	m	.90	m	.90	m	.83
Total	.87	.88	.84	.81	.90	.79	.87	m	.87
SOCIAL IMPACT									
Principals									
Using	.84	.74	.72	.65	.82	.79	.69	.77	.76
Non-using	.80	m	m	.74	.83	.83	.73	.73	m
Total	.83	.73	.74	.72	.84	.82	.70	.75	.76
Teachers									
Using	.83	.81	.80	.75	.81	.78	.79	m	.79
Non using	.85	m	m	m	.81	m	.81	m	.82
Total	.87	.81	.80	.74	.82	.77	.79	m	.80
TRAINING NEED									
Principals								*	
Using	.57	.64	.65	.72	.78	.52	.55	.13	.61
Non using	.67	m	m	.79	.79	.74	.61	.45	m
Total	.62	.63	.70	.75	.79	.64	.56	.33	.61
Teachers									
Using	.66	.65	.68	.76	.77	.69	.65	m	.69
Non using	.81	m	m	m	.80	m	.75	m	.67
Total	.77	.63	.69	.77	.79	.71	.67	m	.69
SELF CONFIDENCE									
Teachers									
Using	.68	.69	.71	.71	.63	.64	.69	m	.71
Non using	.64	m	m	m	.62	m	.58	m	.72
Total	.68	.70	.72	.71	.62	.67	.67	m	.71

Notes. m = less than 25 valid cases. * = alpha reliabilities relatively low, compared to those of other countries on that scale, meaning that one or two of the items in the scale have low or even negative item-total correlation. Further analyses are necessary on those items.

Table F.2
Alpha reliabilities per educational system and category of respondents on attitude scales

Country/Educational System

Scales/Levels	BFL	BFR	CBC	CHI	FRA	FRG	GRE	JPN	LUX	NET	NWZ	POR	SWI	USA
Lower secondary														
EDUCATIONAL IMPACT														
Principals														
Using	.84	.79	.81	.82	.81	m	.72	.87	.75	.76	.79	.75	.75	.80
Non using	.83	m	m	.75	m	m	.93	.82	m	m	m	.84	.81	m
Total	.84	.80	.81	.80	.81	m	.94	.87	.75	.78	.79	.80	.77	.80
Subject teachers														
Using	m	m	.85	m	.85	.81	m	.89	m	.83	.81	.64	.82	.87
Non using	.86	.83	.84	m	.87	.89	.88	.86	.87	.78	.87	.87	.84	.89
Total	.88	.88	.86	m	.88	.87	.88	.88	.87	.81	.86	.85	.85	.89
Computer teachers														
Using	.83	.80	.81	.79	m	.79	.86	.82	.79	.76	.80	.70	.75	.86
Non using	.90	m	m	m	m	m	.86	.85	m	m	m	m	m	m
Total	.86	.81	.80	.79	m	.81	.85	.84	.77	.76	.81	.78	.78	.86
SOCIAL IMPACT														
Principals				*		*								
Using	.82	.82	.64	.56	.74	m	.30	.79	.71	.76	.73	.67	.79	.76
Non-using	.90	m	m	.53	m	m	.61	.77	m	m	m	.67	.80	m
Total	.84	.82	.65	.55	.76	m	.58	.80	.71	.78	.72	.67	.80	.76
Subject teachers														
Using	m	m	.76	m	.77	.79	m	.84	m	.77	.78	.82	.83	.77
Non-using	.87	.75	.81	m	.82	.85	.73	.82	.83	.81	.81	.79	.85	.82
Total	.86	.78	.80	m	.81	.83	.74	.83	.86	.80	.80	.78	.85	.81
TRAINING NEED														
Principals				*							*			
Using	.68	.70	.53	.40	.71	m	.47	.78	.68	.57	.67	.43	.56	.63
Non-using	.64	m	m	.30	m	m	.92	.83	m	m	m	.57	.70	m
Total	.67	.70	.53	.38	.71	m	.93	.80	.68	.58	.66	.49	.63	.63
Subject teachers												*		
Using	m	m	.54	m	.61	.53	m	.76	m	.67	.59	.31	.51	.63
Non-using	.78	.81	.61	m	.67	.67	.82	.79	.88	.66	.62	.41	.57	.71
Total	.76	.79	.59	m	.65	.66	.81	.80	.87	.66	.60	.42	.56	.68
Computer teachers				*						*	*			
Using	.55	.68	.58	.27	m	.52	.48	.65	.67	.31	.67	.10	.28	.54
Non-using	.72	m	m	m	m	m	.45	.65	m	m	m	m	m	m
Total	.58	.68	.56	.25	m	.51	.37	.65	.66	.35	.67	.33	.28	.53
SELF CONFIDENCE														
Subject teachers														
Using	m	m	.45	m	.61	.63	m	.62	m	.73	.75	.60	.63	.66
Non-using	.77	.80	.64	m	.71	.68	.78	.65	.75	.70	.66	.75	.64	.76
Total	.78	.81	.63	m	.68	.69	.78	.65	.77	.73	.69	.69	.65	.74

Notes. m = less than 25 valid cases, * = alpha reliabilities relatively low, compared to those of other countries on that scale, meaning that one or two of the items in the scale have low or even negative item-total correlation. Further analyses are necessary on those items; Scales Social impact and Self confidence for computer education teachers only contained two items and are left out in this table.

Table F.3
Alpha reliabilities per educational system and category of respondents on attitude scales

Country/Educational System

Scales/Levels	BFL	BFR	CBC	FRA	FRG	GRE	HUN	IND	ISR	JPN	NET	NWZ	POL	POR	SLO	SWI	USA
Upper secondary																	
EDUCATIONAL IMPACT										*							
Principals																	
Using	.81	.79	.81	.78	.80	m	.80	.81	.78	.87	.72	.79	.81	.78	.79	.81	.79
Non-using	m	m	m	m	m	.80	m	.82	.80	.79	.44	m	.79	.81	m	m	m
Total	.82	.79	.81	.79	.80	.88	.80	.82	.78	.87	.70	.79	.81	.79	.81	.81	.79
Subject teachers																	
Using	.87	.88	.85	.85	.84	m	.86	.74	m	.88	.86	.87	.75	.73	m	.85	.85
Non-using	.85	.82	.90	.88	.85	.91	.82	.81	.78	.88	.84	.86	.75	.80	.82	.88	.85
Total	.87	.87	.89	.89	.87	.91	.86	.79	.81	.88	.85	.88	.77	.81	.85	.87	.87
Computer teachers																	
Using	.84	.87	.80	.85	.84	.84	.80	.76	.84	.85	m	.82	.79	.75	.90	.85	.87
Non-using	m	m	m	m	m	m	m	.71	m	.89	m	m	m	m	m	m	m
Total	.84	.87	.81	.85	.84	.85	.80	.76	.84	.85	m	.81	.78	.78	.88	.85	.87
SOCIAL IMPACT																	
Principals																	
Using	.82	.84	.64	.74	.82	m	.61	.60	.79	.76	.76	.73	.72	.68	.75	.75	.71
Non-using	m	m	m	m	m	.53	m	.55	.70	.73	.87	m	.70	.65	m	m	m
Total	.82	.85	.65	.75	.82	.56	.63	.58	.77	.76	.80	.73	.72	.67	.70	.74	.71
Subject teachers																	
Using	.85	.80	.79	.77	.74	m	.67	.68	m	.78	.75	.78	.59	.70	m	.74	.81
Non-using	.86	.81	.81	.79	.82	.74	.78	.73	.75	.81	.81	.81	.74	.84	.86	.85	.84
Total	.86	.83	.81	.79	.81	.73	.78	.71	.75	.81	.79	.81	.72	.81	.83	.83	.84
TRAINING NEED																*	
Principals																	
Using	.66	.64	.53	.68	.60	m	.68	.56	.60	.77	.57	.63	.64	.46	.29	.56	.71
Non-using	m	m	m	m	m	.68	m	.50	.72	.86	.66	m	.66	.52	m	m	m
Total	.66	.64	.53	.65	.60	.87	.70	.53	.65	.78	.58	.63	.64	.48	.22	.55	.71
Subject teachers		*												*			
Using	.65	.35	.65	.53	.50	m	.63	.62	m	.69	.62	.54	.53	.37	m	.44	.51
Non-using	.68	.57	.54	.75	.67	.79	.70	.55	.70	.79	.66	.60	.68	.51	.70	.62	.55
Total	.65	.57	.58	.71	.62	.78	.69	.58	.68	.79	.65	.59	.62	.45	.64	.57	.55
Computer teachers		*												*	*	*	
Using	.54	.41	.37	.43	.58	.57	.45	.53	.53	.68	m	.42	.58	.35	.35	.32	.57
Non-using	m	m	m	m	m	m	m	.69	m	.76	m	m	m	m	m	m	m
Total	.53	.42	.36	.48	.58	.51	.45	.55	.54	.70	m	.43	.57	.45	.46	.30	.57
SELF CONFIDENCE					*												
Subject teachers																	
Using	.74	.61	.60	.63	.30	m	.59	.42	m	.67	.69	.56	.46	.48	m	.65	.66
Non-using	.83	.68	.58	.67	.70	.76	.63	.54	.75	.65	.73	.65	.44	.60	.52	.71	.61
Total	.82	.73	.60	.68	.67	.75	.64	.49	.74	.66	.72	.65	.47	.53	.61	.70	.65

Notes. m = less than 25 valid cases, * = alpha reliabilities relatively low, compared to those of other countries on that scale, meaning that one or two of the items in the scale have low or even negative item-total correlation. Further analyses are necessary on those items; Scales Social impact and Self confidence for computer education teachers only contained two items and are left out in this table.

Table F.4
*Alpha reliabilities per educational system and category of respondents
on self-rating scales*

Country/Educational System

Scales/Levels	BFR	CBC	FRA	ISR	JPN	NET	NWZ	USA
Elementary								
KNOWLEDGE INFORMATION TECHNOLOGY								
Teachers								
Using	.83	.83	.82	.66	.84	.81	.81	.84
Non-using	.87	m	m	m	.85	m	.78	.73
Total	.87	.83	.82	.68	.85	.80	.81	.83
PROGRAMMING CAPABILITY								
Teachers								
Using	.89	.82	.78	.76	.83	.86	.78	.84
Non-using	.91	m	m	m	.89	m	.84	.78
Total	.91	.81	.78	.76	.87	.86	.78	.83
CAPABILITY TO OPERATE COMPUTERS								
Teachers								
Using	.86	.76	.75	.79	.82	.81	.76	.82
Non-using	.90	m	m	m	.79	m	.83	.84
Total	.90	.78	.77	.79	.84	.82	.79	.84
TOTAL UNDERSTANDING								
Teachers								
Using	.94	.89	.91	.87	.92	.91	.88	.92
Non-using	.95	m	m	m	.93	m	.91	.89
Total	.95	.90	.91	.87	.93	.91	.89	.92

Note. m = less than 25 valid cases.

Table F.5
Alpha reliabilities per educational system and category of respondents on self-rating scales

Country/Educational System

Scales/Levels	BFL	BFR	CBC	CHI	FRA	FRG	GRE	JPN	LUX	NET	NWZ	POR	SWI	USA
Lower secondary														
KNOWLEDGE INFORMATION TECHNOLOGY														
Subject teachers														
Using	m	m	.80	.84	.82	m	m	.85	m	.86	.86	.84	.83	.83
Non-using	.87	.86	.84	m	.84	m	.90	.85	.74	.86	.83	.81	.84	.79
Total	.88	.88	.84	.84	.85	m	.90	.87	.75	.87	.85	.83	.86	.83
Computer teachers		z	z/*			z/*	z							
Using	.72	.75	.56	.68	m	.57	.65	.84	.76	.72	.80	.74	.64	.71
Non-using	.79	m	m	m	m	m	.62	.85	m	m	m	m	m	m
Total	.77	.74	.54	.70	m	.57	.64	.85	.76	.72	.81	.78	.73	.71
PROGRAMMING CAPABILITY														
Subject teachers														
Using	m	m	.83	.91	.89	m	m	.86	m	.92	.91	.82	.87	.86
Non-using	.92	.89	.88	m	.88	m	.91	.89	.89	.91	.88	.83	.86	.83
Total	.93	.92	.87	.91	.89	m	.91	.90	.88	.92	.90	.84	.88	.85
Computer teachers					*									
Using	.86	.70	.80	.81	m	.74	.56	.82	.81	.82	.87	.76	.79	.79
Non-using	.89	m	m	m	m	m	.53	.87	m	m	m	m	m	m
Total	.87	.67	.83	.82	m	.72	.52	.84	.82	.82	.87	.80	.82	.79
CAPABILITY TO OPERATE COMPUTERS														
Subject teachers														
Using	m	m	.79	.82	.79	m	m	.77	m	.86	.80	.90	.79	.80
Non-using	.91	.88	.85	m	.85	m	.93	.81	.90	.88	.83	.87	.87	.84
Total	.91	.91	.85	.82	.85	m	.93	.85	.91	.90	.83	.88	.88	.83
Computer teachers			*		*									
Using	.79	.80	.34	.75	m	.50	.57	.73	.65	.62	.69	.55	.64	.62
Non-using	.86	m	m	m	m	m	.72	.68	m	m	m	m	m	m
Total	.86	.78	.32	.76	m	.58	.72	.72	.67	.62	.72	.73	.73	.65
TOTAL UNDERSTANDING														
Subject teachers														
Using	m	m	.89	.93	.93	m	m	.92	m	.95	.94	.94	.92	.91
Non-using	.95	.94	.93	m	.94	m	.96	.93	.92	.95	.92	.93	.94	.90
Total	.95	.95	.92	.93	.94	m	.96	.94	.93	.95	.93	.94	.94	.92
Computer teachers														
Using	.89	.90	.70	.84	m	.75	.83	.91	.85	.85	.90	.81	.85	.85
Non-using	.93	m	m	m	m	m	.82	.92	m	m	m	m	m	m
Total	.91	.89	.73	.85	m	.78	.83	.91	.86	.85	.91	.88	.89	.85

Notes. m = less than 25 valid cases, z = zero variance items in scale for this country/category of respondents, * = alpha reliabilities relatively low, compared to those of other countries on that scale, meaning that one or two of the items in the scale have low or even negative, item-total correlation. Further analyses are necessary on those items, z/* = alpha reliabilities relatively low, partly due to zero variance items.

Table F.6
Alpha reliabilities per educational system and category of respondents on self-rating scales

Country/Educational System

Scales/Levels	BFL	BFR	CBC	FRA	FRG	GRE	HUN	IND	ISR	JPN	NET	NWZ	POL	POR	SLO	SWI	USA
Upper secondary																	
KNOWLEDGE INFORMATION TECHNOLOGY																	
Subject teachers																	
Using	.78	.74	.83	.83	.63	m	.80	.74	m	.82	.79	.76	.78	.77	m	.77	.79
Non-using	.86	.81	.86	.84	.85	.89	.83	.88	.85	.86	.83	.80	.83	.84	.85	.83	.79
Total	.86	.84	.85	.86	.87	.90	.86	.86	.87	.87	.83	.82	.84	.85	.84	.85	.81
Computer teachers		z/*		z									*				
Using	.60	.57	.42	.75	.58	.66	.60	.77	.60	.74	m	.63	.52	.72	.68	.66	.73
Non-using	m	m	m	m	m	m	m	.79	m	.80	m	m	m	m	m	m	m
Total	.63	.57	.39	.76	.58	.67	.61	.77	.62	.76	m	.63	.52	.73	.62	.67	.73
PROGRAMMING CAPABILITY																	
Subject teachers																	
Using	.89	.73	.89	.88	.88	m	.86	.78	m	.87	.87	.88	.84	.79	m	.88	.89
Non-using	.93	.87	.90	.88	.93	.90	.89	.90	.91	.91	.89	.88	.84	.84	.90	.90	.87
Total	.93	.89	.90	.90	.93	.91	.91	.89	.91	.91	.91	.89	.86	.83	.88	.91	.88
Computer teachers				*										*	*		
Using	.73	.81	.83	.86	.28	.86	.57	.74	.58	.62	m	.72	.53	.90	.42	.76	.88
Non-using	m	m	m	m	m	m	m	.75	m	.88	m	m	m	m	m	m	m
Total	.75	.81	.85	.86	.28	.81	.59	.74	.57	.72	m	.72	.53	.89	.60	.77	.88
CAPABILITY TO OPERATE COMPUTERS																	
Subject teachers																	
Using	.81	.83	.83	.82	.73	m	.83	.80	m	.79	.82	.69	.77	.80	m	.70	.78
Non-using	.89	.88	.86	.85	.89	.90	.86	.90	.88	.83	.86	.81	.82	.87	.87	.87	.85
Total	.89	.91	.85	.87	.89	.92	.89	.89	.88	.84	.86	.82	.85	.89	.87	.88	.84
Computer teachers				z/*									*				*
Using	.58	.68	.58	.64	.30	.58	.75	.79	.61	.68	m	.45	.60	.74	.76	.55	.42
Non-using	m	m	m	m	m	m	m	.83	m	.79	m	m	m	m	m	m	m
Total	.59	.68	.58	.68	.31	.61	.75	.79	.64	.70	m	.46	.60	.75	.67	.60	.42
TOTAL UNDERSTANDING																	
Subject teachers																	
Using	.91	.90	.92	.93	.88	m	.92	.89	m	.92	.92	.90	.90	.90	m	.89	.91
Non-using	.95	.93	.94	.94	.95	.95	.93	.95	.95	.94	.93	.91	.92	.93	.93	.94	.91
Total	.95	.95	.93	.95	.95	.96	.95	.95	.95	.94	.94	.92	.93	.94	.93	.94	.92
Computer teachers				z													
Using	.79	.79	.77	.86	.61	.76	.83	.89	.76	.85	m	.79	.75	.91	.84	.79	.84
Non-using	m	m	m	m	m	m	m	.92	m	.91	m	m	m	m	m	m	m
Total	.80	.79	.78	.87	.62	.78	.83	.89	.77	.87	m	.80	.75	.90	.81	.81	.84

Notes. m = less than 25 valid cases, z = zero variance items in scale for this country/category of respondents, * = alpha reliabilities relatively low, compared to those of other countries on that scale, meaning that one or two of the items in the scale have low or even negative, item-total correlation. Further analyses are necessary on those items, z/* = alpha reliabilities relatively low, partly due to zero variance items.